Love Among the Lambs

(and other animals too)

by Rosalind Finn

ISBN 978-1466323902

This book is dedicated to the memory of my

gentle shepherd James and our

many years of shared love and laughter.

TABLE OF CONTENTS

BEGIN AT THE BEGINNING ...

—Lewis Carroll (*Alice's Adventures in Wonderland*)

Ovine: meaning of sheep or sheep-like

—Oxford English Dictionary

Only Ewe. Painting by Mikki Colbeck.

FOR TWENTY YEARS, DURING THE 1980S AND '90S, MY HUSBAND JAMES—or, more often, Jim—and I raised sheep on a hill farm in Vermont. This book recounts some of the many stories I have of our lives together during that memorable era.

Jim and I met in Nairobi, Kenya, in 1972. An American who worked for an oil marketing company, Jim had lived and traveled in many countries around the world: Egypt, India, Pakistan, the Middle East, and much of Africa. A highly intelligent man, who, to understand and fully appreciate these temporary homes, Jim had taught himself French, Hindi, a smattering of Arabic and had become fluent in that very lovely language Swahili. He reveled in all the different cultures and was fascinatingly knowledgeable on all manner of subjects. Despite all these achievements, James was, and always remained, one of the humblest people I have ever met.

I was raised in England. I left there in 1960 as an ebullient twenty-one-year-old when I went to visit my grandmother and uncle, who lived in Zimbabwe (or Southern Rhodesia, as it was known in those days). The two months of my scheduled stay in this wonderful country turned into two years until I, eventually, like many restless young people, got itchy feet and felt the need to explore new territory. I drifted northwards to visit cousins living in Kenya. (Ever since an ancestor first emigrated from London to Cape Town in 1820, Africa seems to have been littered with my family members!) I stayed in Kenya for fourteen years, marrying and giving birth to a daughter and a son. I became an avid safari fan and developed especially a lifelong adoration of the often highly flamboyant avian world.

James and I were introduced towards the end of 1974 by a mutual friend. This serendipitous friend invited both of us to that most colonial of meeting places, the well-known Muthaiga Country Club (well known mostly for the wild orgies that had taken place there during the 1920s and '30s among the infamous Happy Valley crowd). Although both Jim and I were in the very unhappy throes of recovering from broken marriages, it was for both of us a classic case of Love at First Sight. A year after our surprise meeting, we were married. And thus commenced a romance that was to fiercely endure for thirty years, until his untimely death and the subsequent sale of our farm.

We were well matched, my Jim and I. He was the patient, quiet, thoughtful one, calmer with our blended family and the many animals we were to be owned by during our marriage. He was a super "Mr. Fix-it" who could turn his hand to most emergencies. One of his main loves in life was carpentry, and when we eventually came to live on the farm, he was never happier than when he was building barns, fences, gates (more about this talent later), or, on rainy or snowy days, just pottering in his well-equipped workshop.

In contrast to Jim's serenity, I was the more mercurial, energetic side of our partnership. A good innovator and idea person, I also organized the general running of the farm and whatever social life we had time for (not much). Both of us shared a deep and abiding love for all creatures, wild and domesticated, and came to deeply appreciate and revere the surrounding landscape.

Our newly married life in Nairobi was fun, with many parties, safaris, friends, and visiting family; sadly, this was not to last for very long. In 1976, Jim's company transferred him to New York, and we settled into a tumbledown old colonial house on the shores of Connecticut. I could write another book about my introduction to America—her strange (to me) and often bizarre (again, to me!) customs, the extraordinary beauty of her countryside, the kindness of her many ethnically varied peoples, my battles with the differences in what is usually presumed to be a "common" language, and, finally, my deepening appreciation for what since has become my own beloved country.

Just as we were once again settling into a new life, the company announced it was moving to Dallas, Texas. A short visit to that city and its environs quickly persuaded us that a move south into yet another new cultural environment would be extremely difficult either for the two of us or our three school-age children, especially with two teenagers in high school and a nine-year-old in elementary school. So Jim accepted the early retirement package offered to employees who didn't wish to move south with the company. We proceeded at once—and as often as possible—to head north to Vermont to look for a new home among that state's verdant pastures and densely wooded mountains.

A year later we found our Shangri-la. It was a lovely two-hundred-year-old white farmhouse perched halfway up a steep hill which went by the name of Grannyhand Hill[1]. The house and surrounding barns were reached by an extremely steep road bordered by ancient maple trees—hence, its most appropriate name of Maple Avenue Farm. So excited were we at the prospect of arriving at the top that we gave little thought to the challenge this road would be in the snowy, icy winters to come (but we found out soon enough).

Surrounding the farmhouse were three big, red, many-tiered barns. Beyond these were ninety-seven wild acres. There was woodland at the very top of this land, in front of which stood an old cowshed, a relic of the farm's long history of dairy farming and, because of its prominent elevation, very much a local landmark. The rest of the landscape consisted of several small copses and much scrubby, uncared-for pastureland, while throughout the whole area meandered moss-covered crumbling stone walls. And most delightfully, hidden among a dip in the hills, a pretty little pond, which was to bring great joy to generations of children in the following summers.

---

[1] Granny Hand was an elderly lady who made hats. One day, while out walking in our woods, we found the ruins of her little cottage.

We moved into our new home one sunny May day a year later, and our new life began. And what a life that turned out to be, especially when we acquired five sheep the following spring.

The sheep buying happened almost accidentally. With so much land to care for, we had discussed in a vague way the best use for it. What about beef cattle? Too large to deal with. Fruit trees? We preferred animals, and the Vermont climate made this idea a bit dicey. Maybe chickens? This was a big "maybe," for while I loved eggs and roast chicken, my attachment to most fowls (except ducks, as I will relate later in this book) stopped there.

A year passed and our conundrum was finally solved, or, as we were many times in the future to conclude, started. We were driving to a neighboring town to meet friends for lunch when we passed a field where a small flock of sheep was grazing. And what sheep! I recognized the breed immediately from my childhood holidays in Scotland—Scottish blackface. With black and white mottled faces, horns (smallish on the ewes, huge and curling on the rams), and thick, creamy fleeces, these animals looked stunningly beautiful against the backdrop of green fields and an intense blue sky. Jim and I turned to each other and with one accord said, "That's it! That's what we need on the farm!"

Thus commenced our husbandry career. Oh, what innocents we were with regards to organizing our new (and extremely wild) ovine population! And we were equally ignorant as to land management and all that that entailed. But my James was, over the following years, to win the respect of the local farmers as he taught himself about farm machinery, fencing, how to return the open land to productive pasture or hayfields, and how to hay those same steep and treacherous fields. For my part, I discovered that I remembered many farming facts learned from my childhood in rural England (my best friend's family ran a dairy/sheep/pig farm), all of which greatly helped us cope with the needs of not only our ever-increasing flock but also all of our other livestock.

Maple Avenue Farm

We learnt that farming is as much about death as about life. That although it was so often a backbreaking and heartbreaking way of life, our newly chosen career also brought us a multitude of triumphs and delights, not to mention a whole lot of hilarity, although this latter was often of the somewhat hysterical variety. We also learnt—and very quickly—that farming (or, be warned, reading about farming!) is not for the faint of heart. However, every one of our animals confirmed my lifetime belief in the beauty, intelligence, and compassion of animals. They taught us about love, patience, equanimity, and endurance, not to mention the quick-wittedness we needed to keep one step ahead of whatever devious plans were being hatched in their animal minds. Perhaps most important of all, husbandry showed us the necessity of keeping our sense of humor at all times. While this book is mainly about raising sheep and the many different aspects of farming that it entails, I didn't feel I could show a complete picture of life at Maple Avenue Farm without including stories about some of the other creatures that figured so prominently in our daily domestic life—our horses, dogs, fowl, honeybees, and so often whatever else might currently be on our "left with us to look after" list—i.e., ducks, mini-horses, a pygmy goat, injured wildlife, etc.

Turn the page and join me for an (in general, but not totally) ovine odyssey.

Fencing – Uphill Work

"Good fences make good neighbors."

—Robert Frost ("Mending Wall")

I TOTALLY AGREE WITH ROBERT FROST. Therefore, my first chapter is not about our livestock but about one of the most important things Jim and I learned during our many years of farming. All too soon after the arrival of our first five sheep, we discovered that while, yes obviously, farming is mostly about animals, fencing is really the first and most essential element for any farm, whether you are aiming to keep your animals in or undesirables out. (It will probably also be a surprise to many readers that while fencing was at the top of our list of to-do's, machinery came in a close second; more about this subject in Chapter Two, "The Mechanics of Farming.") If our sheep ever escaped from their pasture, they could lay waste in double-quick time to a garden (or, even worse, an irate neighbor's garden) and they cared not what sort of garden—flower or vegetable. Strawberry, blueberry, and raspberry patches were much favored, while also at the top of the gourmet list were corn and hayfields in their succulent early growth.

As for keeping undesirables out, that's where a good defense system came in use. Jim and I both believed in trying to live with the natural world rather than destroy it. We found the cruelty of traps totally abhorrent (as we did the hunting of defenseless bears, either with guns or with dogs). We knew there were coyotes in our surrounding woods—and foxes too—who could drag away a newborn lamb, so we made every effort with a variety of barriers to prevent such predators from attacking our flock. Eventually, we were also to invest in a guard llama and a guard dog (more about these two and their uninspiring record of protection later in the book).

However, we were soon to find out, year after year, that fencing has to be the most frustrating, backbreaking, and repetitious of all farm chores. A never-finished task, mending and creating barriers is always high on a farmer's endless to-do list. The face of our land, as I have said, was zigzagged with crumbling stone walls built by early farmers who cleared it to make arable or pasture space and also as a method of restraining their livestock. While these walls made comfortable condominiums for squirrels, chipmunks, and a fascinating variety of insects and beetles, they were not nearly high enough to enclose our feisty flock or our adventure-seeking horses.

When we first moved to the farm and before we became shepherds, the three horses we brought with us were pastured behind bright orange electric tape. It was aesthetically displeasing but serviceable, at least in the warmer months. However, during wintertime, it soon became apparent that the tape didn't work well because heavy snowfalls dragged it down. Of course, our horses were quick to hop over the gap and head downhill for what they supposed was a Better Life.

So our very first spring at Maple Avenue Farm was almost entirely consumed with erecting post-and-rail fences up and down the steep hillsides we had designated as home to our equines. Later, when we decided to go into the sheep business, a whole new array of various kinds of barriers and fences sprouted all over our entire property.

Canny New Englanders know one main thing about putting up fences, and that is that Murphy's Law prevails over this backbreaking task. A fence hole is invariably at least three-quarters excavated when that ominous clang is heard as spade hits stone (or rather, hits huge, immovable Vermont ledge). Consequently, that hole has to be abandoned—and fifteen minutes of hard work with it.

Murphy would certainly have got a load of laughs that first year if he had seen our naïve and inexperienced efforts at fence building! Sweat-soaked and broken-backed, yard by yard we labored on, with only those timeless hand tools to work with—post-hole digger (a tool somewhat like a double spade that opens and closes for gathering up the loose soil at the bottom of the hole), spade, crowbar, old tin can (I preferred using this to the rather cumbersome post-hole digger), hammers and staples, and—definitely most necessary—that friendly sounding tool called the "come-along."

The come-along is a small winch with hooks at either end. After the stock wire (heavy, four-foot-high wire in a grid pattern) has been strung out loosely along the newly installed fence posts, one hook of the come-along is tied to the end of the wire—with baler twine, of course. (Whatever did farmers do before baler twine?) The other hook is attached to a parked truck or convenient tree. Then the winch is ratcheted up until the wire is stretched tight enough against the fence posts for the peons (myself, a nephew, and any unwary friend who might be corralled into helping) to permanently secure it to the uprights with staples. The come-along is then loosened and, voila! there stands a new, beautiful segment of fence line, a truly glorious sight to the hot and tired laborers. During winter, the sight of those straight lines marching through the blue-white snow, matched post for post by their darker shadows, never failed to make my heart sing a little paean of joy.

But Murphy, as usual, had the last laugh. As Jim pointed out each spring, no matter how deep and carefully those posts had been planted, after a few months in the frozen earth, followed by the spring thaw, many of them took on crazy new angles and

…where sheep shall safely graze…

swayed across the hillside like a crowd of drunken bums leaving a bar at closing time. So once again each spring we were faced with the same old task of fixing or rebuilding what we had so laboriously made the previous year.

Then—oh, bliss!—our lives suddenly and dramatically improved (certainly for the peons) during our second year as farmers. We purchased a tractor and, even more important, an auger. An auger is a very large, heavy-duty drill attached to the rear end of the tractor. The machine age had arrived at Maple Avenue Farm and might well be compared to the dawn of the Industrial Revolution in Europe. Joyfully we watched as this miracle implement burrowed rapidly into the brown earth to make a perfect hole in no time at all. It could even break up the dreaded ledge. And if the rock proved too hard even for that powerful drill, why, it was no trouble to start another hole. Our Jack Russell terrier, Bessie, always on the spot during these digging operations as she herself was a champion hole digger (especially in my flower beds), closely watched with a critical eye what she clearly perceived as a fellow excavator at work. Whether the auger came up to her strict standards, she never let us know—professional courtesy, maybe?[1]

We had many "layers" of fences, starting with our far outer perimeters, which were enclosed by the stock fencing with strands of barbed wire stretched tight along the top. This barbed wire helped to deter coyotes that might try scrambling over the fence in search of a tasty lamb dinner. While we were lucky during our farming years not to have any trouble from the regular coyote pack that yipped its way along our borders most nights, every now and again a rogue member became a menace. These loners were more clever and more intent on finding their way through our fencing and barriers than those who worked in a pack.

One March morning when Jim went up to hay the flock, he found to his horror that one of our pregnant ewes had been gruesomely slaughtered and half-eaten during the night. It was especially sad for us as the

---

[1] Poor Bessie—a rather chubby little dog but, nevertheless, not only the aforementioned hole digger but also a great rat catcher—lost her edge one day during a Jack Russell dog show, specifically, the Rat-Catching Competition. (The rats were safely in a cage, so no actual deaths were involved.) The feisty little Russells had to find their way through a network of tunnels to said cage. Bessie was well ahead of all the other dogs when she—most embarrassingly for both of us—got stuck at a sharp corner and had to be dug out, thereby destroying the tunnels and ruining the competition for all the other eager competitors. Both of us slunk away as fast as possible, and I think the only members of this debacle that were happy were the rats.

Fencers at work

dead ewe, Mississippi, had been a bottle-fed lamb and very much a family pet. After this incident, we brought the sheep in every evening to the safety (we imagined) of the barn and its adjacent small pen.

But even this precaution failed us on one occasion. A couple of ram lambs were killed, again during the night and actually right inside what we presumed was an impregnable barrier. I was sure that this time the kill was committed by a cougar. Not only did the killer have to climb an eight-foot-high board fence to get into this particular area—and coyotes don't climb this high—but also, just the day before, while about to turn off the main road onto our lane, I was startled by one of these beautiful and rarely seen cats leaping right in front of my car. The Vermont Fish & Wildlife Department was contacted for an opinion on the slaughter but airily pooh-poohed my sighting. However, after sixteen years in Africa, I know a lion when I see one!

Our real dread, though, was not coyotes but domestic dogs, either singly or in packs. Dogs don't kill for food; they just kill and maim the defenseless sheep for "fun." The resulting carnage is incredibly horrible to see. And dogs, once they get a taste for this "game," will play it again and again. We would have had to pass the matter over to the town, whose legal responsibility is to keep the offending dogs in check, fine the owners, and get them to reimburse us for any dead or injured animals. Thank goodness such a tragedy never happened to us.

To divide our inner pastures, we used five strands of electrified wire with about three thousand volts coursing through it. This could give an unwary victim a painful jolt, especially if said victim was standing in wet grass. Many times did I regret my carelessness in not paying due attention to the location of these live wires, although I lived in hope that the ensuing shocks might serve to stimulate my brain into greater activity. (Sadly, I can't say my theory has produced any results so far.) Our very inmost and most protecting stockade was built onto a room at the back of the barn and had the look of a Wild West fort about it. Built of wide boards, it stood about eight feet high and not only had a couple of barbed wire strands along the top but also between the lower boards. In springtime, within this safe (unless a hungry cougar happened to stop by) haven we kept the ewes and their newborn lambs, until moving them to slightly more roomy accommodations at the front of the barn.

Other lesser forms of fencing included a small, romantic, white picket fence around my flower garden, while the track through the farm was bordered with a white four-board fence. While we were erecting and painting this—and it did look quite fancy—a neighbor dropped by and remarked that four boards were known in Vermont as "rich man's fencing." Unfortunately, that adage never did come true for us.

Important as the fences were, gates interspersed between them were equally relevant as we were always needing to move our flock between pastures. We had metal gates, wooden gates, and Vermont gates. The latter (I'm not sure why they are called Vermont gates as I can also remember them from my childhood in England) served as a kind of quick fix in an emergency but tended to hang around for years because there was never time to replace them with a sturdier model. These Vermont gates were used along the electric wiring or stock fencing. Jim first cut vertically through the stock wire or electric strands next to a fence post (having, of course, first turned off the current running through it). The resultant loose ends were then wound around a stout pole that was held in place against the fence post by two wire loops, one each at its top and bottom.

Lastly, for humans to make easy transitions between fields, he built old-fashioned wooden stiles. When using these, I always felt like someone from a Jane Austen novel, and I really wouldn't have minded if Mr. Darcy had appeared striding out of the mist to chat me up!

When it came to building these gates, my husband was a true professional. The only difficulty with his finished works was their size, which tended to be massive, with corresponding weightiness. I vividly remember one winter when, working in the warmth of the sheep barn for a couple of months, he finished a really huge and splendid eight-foot-long by six-foot-high creation of very solid pine. When the day came to hang it, two dilemmas presented themselves. Firstly, this gate was so heavy we had to find a couple of friends to come and help us lift it.[2] Our second, and more disastrous, problem only became apparent as we all staggered awkwardly towards the door with our huge burden. The awful realization dawned upon us that the

---

[2] The fact that I had just had a major operation three weeks earlier was lightly dismissed. Farmers' wives are never allowed to admit to weakness of any sort and are always expected to do their share of lifting and hauling, no matter what the circumstances.

gate was too big to fit through the barn door. Unfortunately, this was not one of those large double doors found at the front of most barns. It was just a little old-fashioned side exit, no higher than five feet. The story of the camel not being able to go through the eye of the needle came vividly to mind as the air around me buzzed with some very warm language from my husband.

Various solutions were put forward, some not particularly useful, such as knock down the whole bloody barn; knock down only the outside wall; knock down the doorway; or—and here, finally and thankfully, common sense started to take over—dismantle the whole damn gate and rebuild it outside. In view of the age of the barn, it was decided not to interfere with it in any way and risk a wholesale collapse of said building, and so the last solution was ultimately, with grudging acceptance, decided upon.

Some weeks later, as the maple trees along our avenue started to take on a delicate pink hue, this infamous structure was hung grandly from very high and very solid posts along our stockade wall, where it daily received the admiration it deserved, although not from the sheep with their ever constant desire to escape any and every enclosure.

Our flock, as might be imagined, appreciated neither our gates nor our fencing. The ovine motto must surely be, "The grass is always greener on the other side of the fence." No matter how lush was any new field they were turned out into, our sheep spent hours trudging up and down their barriers to check if, by some wild chance, a gap had been left in the defenses. At last, defeat was conceded, at least temporarily, as the need to lie down and do some cud chewing became vital. But let the electricity stop running through the wires for any reason—Jim making Vermont gates, a thunderstorm, or a short caused by a branch falling somewhere onto the wire—and our ewes knew it instantly. And if the wires were too tight or too low for the mothers' large wooly bodies to get through, why, the next best thing was to get their lambs under. On several occasions, during times when the wires were not hot, Jim actually saw Emerald, one of our older, bolder, and shrewder mothers, lift up the lowest wire with her horn so that her baby could slip into my vegetable garden—and I constantly meet people who tell me sheep are stupid!

A well earned break; Bessie supervising the donuts.

On precipitous slopes such as ours, the erection of fences, particularly wire ones, required ingenuity. As it can be very difficult to get the bottom strand really taut, Jim and I developed a singular, if unorthodox, way to solve this problem. I would lie flat on my back, with my two feet holding the bottom of the wire in place against the fencepost. Jim, his back to the fence, then straddled my supine body and hammered home the staples from between our legs.

One warm spring day as we were working together far up on the hillside, we heard a visitor calling from the farmyard below. At our answering "halloo," she moved into our view and I could see her trying to locate us somewhere high above. As she marked our position, I saw her falter a little. Was she intruding on an intimate moment, maybe some weird shepherds' ritual or even—terrifyingly—a murder? Despite our second cry of welcome, she turned and quickly disappeared down into the valley again. Later, when I tried to explain what we were actually doing, I don't think she believed me. It seems everyone has heard that sheep farmers are known to have some inexplicable customs.

One especially dry summer, we started to run out of viable pasture for the flock. At the bottom of our land there was an area of about two acres that had been left as scrubland. There were a few larger trees growing there, but most of it was brambles, overgrown grasses, and saplings. Rough pasture as it was, but growing desperate for more grazing area, we hoped that even this terrain might serve to ease our problem. But we needed to use it immediately, and with only the two of us, it would take at least two or three weeks to fence in.

Having just read an article about Amish barn raisings, an idea struck me. What about a fence-raising day? Luckily for us, Jim came from a very large family; in fact, he had forty-one nephews and nieces, many of whom lived in New England. An urgent SOS was issued, and many of them, being a friendly and helpful clan, managed by the following weekend to turn out—no fewer than twenty-one workers to help us with our huge task.

Jim and I spent the week before the event getting organized by gathering the appropriate materials and tools and formulating an all-important Plan of Action. Early in the morning of the appointed day, our family and many local friends gathered and were assigned their various tasks. First off the mark came the designation of weed whacker, whose job it was to clear away grass and small shrubs along the line of prospective fencing. Next was a person lugging a heavy bucket of lime and an eight-foot measuring stick. A small pile of the white lime was deposited every eight feet to show where the fence posts were to be planted. Then came the big machinery: tractor with, naturally, its attached auger and manned by two or three strong nephews; truck with fence posts aboard; the workers responsible for settling in the posts; and, almost last, a second, borrowed truck containing the fencing wire. At the very end of the line straggled a lowly bunch of workers armed with hammers and staples.

Family at work, Fred leading the crew

We had staying with us at that time a very pretty English girl by the name of Emily. She was not only an extremely hard worker but also bountifully endowed by nature with a spectacular body. Since it was a hot August day, Emily became more and more scantily attired as she toiled along in the final hammer-and-staples gang. The day wore on and the working order gradually and extraordinarily changed. Late morning found the tractor and truck crews, which, of course, had by some strange masculine logic all been young males, were now working at the back of the line with our resident Venus. This meant some of the women—to their delight—were able to leave the backbreaking task of hammering in the wire to take over driving the vehicles. Not surprisingly, Emily became the most popular member, not only of the male half of the workforce but of its female half too.

Lunch break saw us all lounging comfortably in the shade of a small copse while we gulped down glasses of tart homemade lemonade. The delicious and reviving chili that followed was the contribution of a helpful friend to our fence-raising day. After this meal and a short rest, we slowly and a lot more heavily wended our way back to work. By 4:00 p.m., as the sun started to dip towards the high western hills, the last staple was hammered in and a satisfied cheer rang out. In our hot, sweaty, and exhausted state, we all repaired to our cool front porch, and never did a cold beer taste so good.

The poet Jacques Delille once said, "Fate chooses our relatives, we choose our friends." But whenever I think upon the incredible achievements of this fence-raising day, I know I am thankful to each one of these remarkable family members and dear friends for their unstinting love and help. They're all certainly the best fence raisers in New England.

Agnes (at rear) and Teddy

Agnes and Beaver

Shortly after settling into our new home, we visited friends who bred Scottish deerhounds, large and gentle dogs whose joy in life is to run in huge, leaping bounds across open meadows. We instantly fell in love with a three-month-old bitch puppy, and thus entered dear Agnes into our lives. She was named after an aunt of Jim's, as he said Agnes's perpetually mournful expression reminded him vividly of that rather sad woman. Luckily, this was the only characteristic that our wonderful dog shared with Auntie Ag.

Indeed, Agnes, as she grew to maturity, was anything but unhappy. In fact, when she came into season for the first time, she turned out to be quite a "hottie," and we were hard pressed to keep her from running off to find an unsuitable lover. When she was eighteen months old and came into heat for the second time, we decided to let her have one litter of puppies before spaying her. We picked out the perfect mate: a tall, dark, and handsome deerhound called Edward—Teddy, for short. He conveniently lived in the next town and was booked to come over and meet Agnes when her fertility was at its peak.

Since we had not actually seen any unwanted male suitors during Agnes's first heat, we presumed that because our farm was situated high on a hillside and quite far away from other habitations, we didn't need to be so careful this second time. We were right—more or less. Her only lover turned out to be an amorous and hopeful Jack Russell terrier, obviously possessed of a terrific sense of smell since he lived two miles away! Upon his panting and eager arrival, I telephoned his family and asked them to come and collect him.

"We'll be there pronto," came the reply, "but I don't think you have to worry too much. Agnes is very tall and Beaver is very short."

But I, having known the wily ways of dogs all my life, quickly replied, "Don't be too sure. Remember that Russells are very ingenious and determined little dogs and we live on a very steep hillside!"

Poor Beaver was ignominiously removed, and in due course the glamorous Teddy arrived to do his duty. And nine weeks later, Agnes was delivered of ten beautiful puppies, none of them, thank goodness, with Jack Russell markings.

THE MECHANICS OF FARMING

On mechanical slavery, on the slavery of the

machine, the future of the world depends.

—Oscar Wilde (The Soul of Man under Socialism)

WHY DID I EVER THINK THAT FARMING was about livestock or agriculture? How could I have been so wrong? Forget the sheep, cows, pigs, corn, hay, or whatever. After a year at Maple Avenue Farm, enlightenment finally dawned: farming was about none of the above. It was about machinery. Machinery, great and small, simple and complicated, mostly very noisy and very costly. Farming is the greatest excuse in the world for men to have large, greasy, smelly toys to play with.

First in a long line of mechanical objects to arrive on our, at that time, fledgling sheep farm (or "ranchette," as a Southern friend once described it) was a big GMC three-quarter-ton flatbed truck. Jim then enclosed the flatbed with wooden sides and two gates at the rear for loading and unloading. It proved very useful for moving around livestock, furniture, and shavings, and taking old scrap metal (of which, as on most old farms, there was a plethora strewn all over the fields and woods and in the barns) to the recycling center. In fact, even Jim's mother-in-law, while on a visit from England, was once honored with a ride in the back. And Jim could at last be a member of the local Trucking Fraternity and give other passing truckers the correct salute: the laconic lifting of the index finger from the steering wheel, accompanied by an equally laconic nod of the head.

There's another quick story attached to passengers in the truck. Our deerhound, Agnes, was in fact the most privileged passenger of all and accompanied Jim wherever he drove. Agnes (and Jim) knew all the best stops—Dunkin' Donuts, the bank (dog biscuits came out in the cash drawer), McDonald's, and, most favorite, Sandy's Drive-in in Sharon for an ice cream. One day, a neighbor who lived at the bottom of the hill asked me where Jim and I had been going the previous afternoon. "I didn't go anywhere with Jim yesterday," I replied. "I was out of town until late evening." Then who…and I laughed. It was Agnes my curious friend had seen sitting happily beside Jim. Well, although the dog and I shared grey hair, I never thought my nose was quite that long or my ears quite that pointy!

A truckload of sheep

Jim's next purchase was a very small ancient tractor. Ancient it might have been, but totally beloved and cherished by my husband. He even bestowed a name upon this green machine: Trackie Boy. Jim was aided in his purchase of the truck and the following farm machinery by Ralph Brown, one of our close neighbors who lived at the bottom of the hill.

Ralph was a retired dairy and pig farmer, a wonderfully kind man who was a most welcome adviser to our nascent farming efforts. Like many Vermont farmers, Ralph was somewhat stern of face on first meeting, but when we got to know each other better he turned out to have a very lively sense of humor. When cracking a joke, his blue eyes (why do so many Vermont farmers have those bright blue eyes—reflection of the sky, perhaps?) would twinkle and a slow smile would spread across his usually deadpan face.

For a while, the tractor and the truck were all that we needed for our daily life because Jim had not yet learned the art of haying. That was taught us—or rather, taught to Jim particularly—by another farmer neighbor, Gile Kendal. He came over to cut our fields for us in our first summer.

This eighty-year-old Vermonter obviously felt more at home on a tractor than anywhere else. What a joy it was to watch him—old hat jammed low on his head, cigar sticking out of the corner of his mouth, body hunched over the steering wheel, moving in perfect time with the lurching and bumping of his machine. The fact that our farm was situated on a very steep hillside deterred Gile not a whit. He mowed everything, and I mean everything, regardless of the cant of the slope. If it was green and growing, it was cut, raked, tedded, and baled by Gile. I conceived a huge respect for this skillful old farmer and once again became aware that although one can acquire a degree by the traditional college route, there are a myriad of different ways to become a Master of Arts.

In the January of our second year, we decided that we had enough basic skills to tackle the following summer's haying season by ourselves. Of course, in order to facilitate this, we would need more machinery. In fact, quite a variety of it. The most important item to start with was a bigger, stronger tractor. This was a serious piece of shopping for Jim. After weeks of research that involved much brochure perusing, countless miles—and as many hours—going to view different models[1] of machines, and endless discussions with other members of the Tractor Fraternity, Jim settled for a John Deere, model 1050.

On the day of its arrival, the barn was swept clean and, because there was only room for one machine in this now sparkling shelter, the old tractor, looking very forlorn, was parked outside with a tarpaulin over it, as if covering its shameful antiquity. Poor Trackie Boy. I asked, tongue-in-cheek, if there was to be a red carpet laid down for the advent of this modern marvel, but no reply was deemed necessary to such a facetious remark. At last, with much loud grinding of gears, toiling up our hill came a huge truck and trailer holding Jim's new green, glowing machine. Peace reigned over the farm, and I hardly saw my husband for the next week as he fussed around this latest acquisition, poured over its outer and inner workings, and buried himself every evening in its tome-like instruction manual.

---

[1] There's an amusing anecdote attached to the word "models." At this time of machinery buying, so deeply immersed was I in thoughts of different ilks of sheep that I once asked a farmer friend what "breed" of tractor he owned. Needless to say, he gave me a very quizzical look.

Following this grand event, I, in my ignorance, thought that after this huge investment we would take a break from machinery purchases. Hah! I hadn't reckoned with the need for the essential haying parts. Any self-respecting tractor, not to mention tractor owner, requires lots of these: front parts, back parts, parts to pull, parts to push—the list is endless. Over the following months, our farmyard began to look like a used machinery lot. Before plunging into the extravaganza of haying equipment, Jim bought some other tractor add-ons that he obviously felt he could not do without: a front-end loader with eight ferocious-looking, two-foot-long "teeth"; the auger mentioned in Chapter One; and an implement that fitted to the tractor's rear end, called a brush hog. This was a sort of large, very strong mowing device used for cutting tough brush and grass in areas where hay isn't grown but needs to be kept under some sort of control.

Our bank balance sank lower and lower.

This seemingly endless list came to a temporary halt with the final salute to glory—the various parts that made up the haying team. Shopping for these things involved assiduous attendance at farm sales. I was struck by what became a familiar scenario: farmer meandering slowly along rows of often incomprehensible-looking machinery, followed by a bored-looking wife clutching her large pocketbook containing the where-withal to pay for the carefully chosen purchase. (I often wished there was a tent in one corner of the sales field to which we wives could repair and have a lot more fun drinking martinis while waiting to be sum-moned to hand over the cash!) After a few weeks of intense looking, we managed to put together the whole shebang: mower, tedder, rake, and—the grand old man of them all—a baler.

Our bank balance teetered precariously between red and black.

Of all the equipment on our farm, I have always particularly had the greatest respect for balers. Even after years of watching them at work in the hayfields, I still find this machine miraculous. The baler is attached to the back of the tractor by a long metal shaft (quite like an umbilical cord), which can sway in a stiff way to accommodate the movements of its host machine. Down the raked rows this cumbersome assemblage advances. First, the raked hay is sucked into the baler's maw. Then, amidst great churnings and clankings

Trackie Boy the Second in action – Bessie supervising.

and sometimes the odd, heartfelt groan, the hay is pushed into a series of flat wads, called flakes, that are compressed into a bale about two feet long. Next comes the really clever part of the proceedings: twine is stretched around the bale in two places and knotted tightly by a couple of little arms. Finally, the neatly packaged bale is slowly and triumphantly squeezed from the rear of the baler and dropped onto the field to await transport to the barn.

I was slow to realize after the arrival of all this equipment that I was about to become that well-known farming figure: a tractor widow. Jim practically slept with his new acquisitions. He certainly dreamt about them night and day. In fact, he identified with them so closely that I was a little muddled when one morning he came into the kitchen and announced dramatically, "My plunger went through my wad board."

"Oh, good heavens!" I said. "Are you all right? Where do you hurt? Shall I call the Fast Squad?"

"What on earth for? I'm okay. It's my wad board that's broken."

"Well, I thought it was a strange part of you I hadn't heard of before. So is it part of the tractor?"

"No, no. It's a vital part of the baler," said Jim. "Could you call Saint Ralph and see if he can make an emergency call?"

Every spring, Ralph Whitney (or, as Jim and I called him, Saint Ralph, Patron Saint of Balers) visited all the area farms and laid his skilled hands upon our balers, which then, without fail, worked with well-oiled precision all summer. This Ralph, like our friend Ralph Brown, seemed to appear quite reserved at first introduction, but he warmed up over time and even became quite talkative after a couple of baler visits. This time, as always, he quickly answered our plea for help, fixed both plunger and wad board, and haying resumed. How lucky we were to have on call a man of such mechanical prowess.

Over the years, our ownership of machinery grew. We bought a small trailer, originally built to transport mini horses, to take our sheep to state fairs and to new owners; an ancient but serviceable ATV, useful for transporting fencing and carpentry tools to outlying sites of the farm; and a gas-driven weed whacker, somewhat like a heavy-duty lawnmower. This last machine could operate in the smaller areas of the sheep pens and stable yards and was great for getting rid of horrible invasive plants, like burdocks, gill over the ground, rhubarb (yes, great for pies, but how many pies can you eat?), nettles, and thistles.

With the advent of the machine age at Maple Avenue Farm, I found that I not only had to learn a whole new vocabulary, but in some ways I also had to adapt to yet another new way of life.

Taking mother for a spin on the ATV.

Besides being a tractor widow, I also was quickly apprised of the fact that like any good farmer's wife, I was always expected to stop immediately whatever I might be doing, however important it might be to me, if any equipment broke down, especially during the haying months. I became adept at dropping whatever chore I was trying to accomplish and rushing over to the John Deere store in South Royalton for such extraordinary-sounding things as clevis pins, billhooks, and dog springs, not to mention the aforesaid wad board.[2] But I've always felt that it's good to have one's knowledge base expanded, even to include a cache of tractor parts!

---

[2] Clevis pins, billhooks, dog springs, and wad boards are all parts (still mysterious and complicated to me) that go into making a hay baler work. They help to push the hay into the compartment where it is compressed into an oblong shape, tied with baler twine, and spat out as a bale of hay.

With most of our machinery in almost perpetual motion, we were constantly aware of trying to operate it at maximum safety levels. As any insurance company will tell you, a great percentage of bad accidents happen on farms and involve farm vehicles. We were very particular about who rode our ATV or operated the weed whacker or tractors. But, as previously mentioned, Murphy's Law tends to prevail over even the most cautious.

One summer's day, we had a mishap of a rather strange nature. We'd been haying our topmost field. The truck had just departed slowly down the steep hill with the season's final load of hay for the barn below. Our young crew was jubilant. It had been a hard, hot afternoon and the chaff had stuck to and was pricking their sweaty bodies, increasing the general discomfort of the work. As we bumped out of sight, Jim, who was always the most careful of men (I was usually the absent-minded one of us), found a small flattish—though there was nothing really flat anywhere among our hills—plateau and parked the weary tractor and baler. Quickly he dismounted, having an extremely urgent need to answer a call of nature.

However, what with the elation of finishing the long and arduous gathering in of the hay crop and the almost unbearable pressure on his bladder, my husband's usual caution had forsaken him, and although he had thought to leave the machinery in as safe a position as possible, in his haste he had, unfortunately, forgotten to put on the tractor's brake. As he stood relieving himself while admiring the magnificent view stretched out below, his mighty-wheeled Bucephalus—to his horror—began to creep forward. Now, as every-one knows, nature has not designed our bladders, especially men's, to stop in midstream. So there stood poor James, helplessly transfixed as the two machines started inching slowly downhill. As the slope steepened, the tractor rushed faster and faster, swerving from side to side, bumping over the newly shorn field, breasting hummocks with glee, the baler yanked willy-nilly behind it. One could almost imagine the tractor shouting, "Yippee!" at its newfound freedom after weeks of heaving, slogging labor.

Meanwhile, we were busy stacking the bales into the barn when it gradually dawned on us that something peculiar was happening on the hill above. Loud clanking noises echoed down to us, coupled with the occasional shout from Jim. All at once, a stupendous crash resounded through the air. Even the sheep stopped grazing to raise inquiring heads. Then silence, heavy and ominous, fell over the farm. Slowly and quietly we climbed back uphill.

In a steep, wooded area between the upper and lower hayfields, the tractor, Jim's pride and joy, lovingly embraced a stout tree. Behind it, still attached, although now at a grotesque angle, lay the baler. Behind both was my husband, executing a kind of war dance of mortification.

A kind and sympathetic neighbor was contacted to help pull out both machines and drag them down to the farmyard. The tractor would have to be hauled away to the "hospital" in South Royalton, and I was instructed to telephone immediately for Saint Ralph about the baler. When I told him of the accident, he sounded—for Ralph—very excited. Obviously, this was going to be a challenge, perhaps the challenge of a lifetime. Less than an hour later I heard his old truck grind its way round behind our barns.

Reluctant to intrude on what might be a situation fraught with agony, I waited some time before wandering up to see how things were going. Ralph had his head deep into the inner workings of our injured machine, with Jim, like a surgeon's assistant, hovering anxiously beside him and handing over spanners and other small tools. When I asked (cautiously and with great trepidation, because I didn't really want to know the answer) how things were going, the surgeon looked up and, with the greatest disappointment in his voice, informed me that he "reckon(ed) it wasn't all that bad." Well, poor Ralph's challenge might have evaporated, but my husband and I were mighty glad of his verdict.

In time, Jim had both of his beloved machines restored to him in perfect working order, and serenity, at least temporarily, reigned over our farm once more

Phillip and Jemima courting

Ducks and Johnnie

At some unremembered time, we gave a home to a pair of Pekin ducks. The male we called Phillip, after our daughter's current boyfriend, and the female, of course, became Jemima Puddleduck. How elegant these two birds were, with their deep creamy yellow plumage and bright orange feet and beaks.

Phillip and Jemima were a very devoted couple and waddled happily around the farm and barns all day, wack-wacking to each other as they discussed the various delicious tidbits they found in the manure pile or maybe in the depth of the puddles dotting the farm tracks after a rainfall.

Phillip was a brave bird and very protective of his wife. One day, Johnny, one of Agnes's grown sons who had stayed on with us, thought it might be fun to tease the little drake and his wife by playfully barking and lunging at them. What a shock poor Johnny got! Phillip, spreading his wings and stretching his neck to its most extreme length, rushed at the huge dog and pecked viciously at Johnny's most vulnerable underparts. With a howl of pain, the huge hound fled the scene with undignified haste. And what a lesson was learned that day by all the other watching canines: don't mess with this fowl couple!

Rites of Spring

Baa, baa, black sheep,

Have you any wool?

Yes sir, yes sir,

Three bags full.

—Anonymous

I'VE ALWAYS LIKED THE PHRASE "THE RITES OF SPRING." It conjures up visions of fragile maidens clad in wispy chiffon, dancing over misty meadows. All of which is very romantic to dream about, but on our farm, the rites were a lot more prosaic.

Several tasks needed attention at the end of March. One was checking my beehive. With great trepidation, I approached the hive and gave it a discreet knock. If this produced an instantaneous and angry buzzing from inside, my heart would sing; they had survived the winter! Off I would run to mix up some sugar water for their temporary sustenance. Although in the fall I always tried to make sure the hive had adequate honey supplies to carry them through the long winter months, if spring came late (as is often the case in Vermont) and their honey was all eaten up, the hive could starve to death. But spring in our northern climes is the hardest of all times for honeybees because if cold or very rainy weather delays the blooming of maple buds or spring blossoms, then the hive is in very real danger of dying of starvation. The sugar water can at least keep them going until warmer, sunnier days arrive.

Other creatures also needed attention at this time of year. The three horses had to have their yearly check-ups and shots from the vet, and hoof trimming from the farrier. Our four (usually this number, but on occasion as many as six or seven) dogs also needed their canine shots, and what a black day on the dog calendar that was. Although I would try to disguise the car ride to the vet clinic as an outing to the feed store, when we left the highway at a different exit, I could feel suspicion starting to emanate from the crowded back seat. Shortly thereafter, the shivering began as my final betrayal became apparent and the House of Horror was arrived at. I won't go into the embarrassment that ensued for me as each dog was dragged unwillingly inside, especially when it was the turn of Bessie, the Jack Russell. Anyone who has ever had experience with a member of this feisty little breed will know that they can produce a particularly shrill and agonized scream, even though nothing painful has actually happened to them as yet. It was just a kind of terrier objection.

And an extremely loud one! For a couple of days after the trip, I was studiously ignored by all the victims as punishment for their horrendous experience.

Next on the spring to-do list, when the snow had finally sunk into the ground, were the fence lines. All of these needed to be checked to see how many posts had been heaved out of the ground, or partly so, by deep frost. The tractor, although it had not been idle during the winter when it was needed for pushing snow away from the barns and off the track through the farm, seemed to develop a spring in its wheels as the auger was attached. Merrily it set off up the farm track, with Jim, also bursting with spring fever and singing at the top of his voice, on board.

But by far the most important springtime events on a sheep farm were shearing and lambing. Shearing came first and took place in the last week of March. Our shearer, David Hinman, with his skill and gentleness, was much in demand among shepherds all over New England and beyond. One year, he even traveled to Peru to learn how to shear llamas, a trip that turned out to be a bonus for us and our llama, Lloyd. We always booked David's visit a year in advance to be sure he could be with us at our chosen time.

The night before the big day, the whole flock—with the breeding ewes, the yearling ewes, and the rams, usually comprising around thirty animals altogether—was shut in the barn to make sure they were kept dry and that they were ready and waiting for David's arrival. If rain or snow seemed at all likely any time the week before his visit, they might be shut in for several days; it's impossible to shear wet wool. While the placid rams gave us no trouble and were perfectly content to settle into the barn with fresh hay and water, our ewes, always troublesome and unhappy with any change in their routine, were a different story. They loved the outside life and objected loudly to being herded into the dark reaches of our old barn. Pushing and shoving each other, they generated a terrific volume of complaints. While this cacophony quieted down overnight, when we arrived at the barn with David next morning to start work, the irate fretting started up as forcefully as ever.

Shearing day was popular among our friends, and we never lacked willing volunteers to help us. As with our fence-raising day, shearing time also took on a somewhat sexist appearance. Jim, his male helpmates, and David worked with the sheep inside, while I and my women companions attended to the newly shorn fleeces outside on the barn porch.

To start the barbering process, David first had to set up and oil his electric shears, while outside on the barn porch we women erected the wool bag. This was a seven-foot-long hopsack bag (now, sadly, modernized to plastic) that was hung inside a tall metal scaffold. An old door balanced across two trestles served as the sorting table, where we cleaned up the newly shorn fleeces.

Everything now in readiness, the great moment came to start work. The first reluctant ewe was dragged into the presence of her barber. It might be noted that as the first victim disappeared through the door, the steady baa-ing racket from our "girls" ceased at once and was replaced by a palpable unease that rippled through the waiting clientele. They knew Something Nasty was going on. But as Dave gently turned the protesting ewe onto her side, her struggles ceased and she went completely limp and silent, allowing him to do his work without hin-

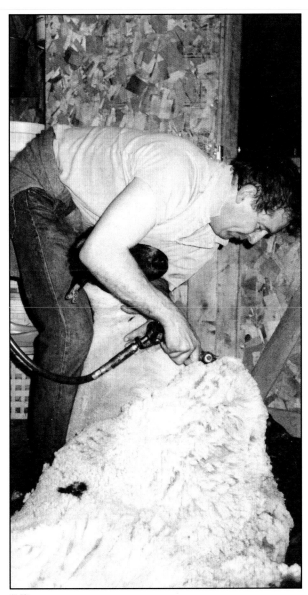

Off it comes!

drance. There were none of these wild shenanigans with the farm's more docile rams, who submitted meekly to this loss of wool.

The haircut commenced. How I loved that first long swoop of the shears down the back of the recumbent sheep! The movement had such beauty to it, enhanced by the creamy foam of wool that gradually parted company with its owner. While the back area was cut off with several long passes, the neck, tail, and belly areas required more detailed and delicate cutting. A skilled operator like David took the entire fleece off in one piece and left no cuts or nicks on the animal in the process. When the fleece lay in a supine pile on the floor, David would then give the bare ewe her yearly shot against tetanus before releasing her to bound back amongst her silent and nervous sisters. For the most part, the bare ewes always looked fat and fit, and my Jim would stand beaming with pride as David complimented him on the good condition of his beloved flock. The whole operation took about ten minutes. Although I am sure in Australia and New Zealand, where they have thousands of sheep to shear in a short time, fleecing a sheep is a very much faster procedure, but (luckily for us) with our small flock, David could perform his task in a slower, gentler way.

Tana the mini-sheep off for a much needed haircut.

By the end of March our ewes were all in an advanced stage of gestation. Once naked, we could take a good look at them and estimate by the size of their udders how soon each would be lambing. Sometimes these expectant mothers had such huge bellies that I mentally put them down as expecting triplets. Although it is slightly stressful for a ewe to be shorn at this late stage of pregnancy, it poses less of a problem than a newborn lamb sucking on the mother's long wool instead of her nipple. One year we did have a ewe whose waters broke while under David's ministrations. Half an hour later she produced a

Setting up the woolbag, Bessie supervising.

healthy lamb, and neither mother nor baby seemed any the worse for their experience.

We always had to remember to issue a warning to David when it was the turn of our wether, Zircon, on the shearing floor. Wethers are castrated rams. Because of their calm temperament, they are often kept with the females to be flock leaders. They have much shorter horns than their intact male brethren, and as they lack testicles to announce the presence of a penis (hidden in thick wool), there was always a real danger that our shearer would mistake Zircon for a ewe and sever this very important organ! This actually did happen to a wether belonging to a friend of ours. By a real stroke of luck, she was able to locate a veterinarian on a call just down the road. The vet rushed over and stitched the vital part back onto its owner. This wether lived for many more years and never suffered any ill effects from his Bobbitt-like experience.

While the men's work was going on in the barn, outside (hopefully, in sunshine) we women found plenty to occupy ourselves. As each fleece was shed, it was handed out to us across the Dutch door, our hands getting a free beauty treatment from the wool, still warm and greasy with lanolin from its recent owner. It was laid out on the sorting table, and we picked off all the chaff and dirty wool—known as 'tags'. These were then put into a special bag, which I used very effectively for mulching my summer garden. Fleece cleaned, it was rolled up and tossed into the wool bag. When the bag got about half full, a child was co-opted into climbing up the scaffold, jumping into the bag, and tamping down the wool inside. Small children disappeared completely, and hauling them out of the hopsack was a lot more difficult than getting them in!

At midmorning, we stopped for a short coffee and cookie break to ease David's back and catch up with news of his family and his past year's activities. While hanging around chatting, we watched with great amusement the flock's reaction to their sudden strange nudity. They all now looked a little top-heavy, especially the rams, whose huge horned heads seemed quite out of proportion to their suddenly smaller bodies. On the whole, it appeared to be quite a relief for them to be free of their thick shaggy coats, which I think got quite itchy with the coming of warmer weather, and there was much rubbing and scratching along the fences and against the hay feeders. There was also a certain amount of critiquing of each other's new hairdos and, judging by some of the head tossing that went on, not all of it complimentary. I so wished I understood "ovine-ese" so that I could be in on what was being said.

Finally, the last fleece was thrown into the wool bag and we moved on to the very dramatic event of shearing our llama, Lloyd. Unlike sheep, llamas, thankfully, only need to be shorn once every two years. I don't know whether we—or Lloyd, for that matter—would have had the strength to endure this crazy ordeal every year. He was a camelid of very confirmed opinions, and he didn't like David wielding the shears in such close proximity to his body. Amid much spitting and rolling of eyes, the poor creature was dragged onto the shearing floor and firmly grasped by four brave (or perhaps foolhardy?) helpers. Jim then draped a large blanket over Lloyd's head. This act, while it stopped the outpouring of spittle, did little to lessen the struggling of our besieged friend, and the llamaic swearing, although now muffled, didn't cease for a minute.

Will I be able to get out?!

This was one of those times when David realized that speed, not skill, was of the essence if he was to get the job done before all hell broke loose. The soft brown wool fell swiftly to the floor and the barbering was over in a few minutes. Equally quickly, the door was opened, captors scattered to a safe distance, the blanket whisked away, and Lloyd would shoot outside like a bird startled from its nest. He looked even stranger than his ovine friends, and it took the poor fellow days to recover from this insult to his person.

All that was left to do after this lively interlude was to take down the bursting wool bag and sew it closed with baler twine, after which it was dragged into the back of the barn to await transport to the wool pool sale during the summer months. The scaffold and the table were collapsed and loaded into David's truck, and he was gratefully paid. Arm in arm, Jim and I watched as his vehicle disappeared down our steep hill— farewell until next year. In the pen, our flock, rapidly getting used to their new nakedness, was relaxing over their morning hay. To their weary but very satisfied caretakers, they looked beautifully sleek, although most of them by no means slim!

Another rite of spring was over, and while the sheep might be taking time off, there was no time for Jim and myself to do likewise. We had to hurry and begin preparations for our next and (for me) most exciting event of the year—lambing!

Ilka and Rudyard

Rudyard the cat and his friend Ilka

When we arrived at Maple Avenue Farm, we brought three horses with us. During the ensuing years, we were gifted with several others. Perhaps my most beloved of these gifts was a most beautiful white Trakehner mare, called Ilka.

What a blessing was this gentle, kind, and loving horse, especially for children and nervous riders. Trained as a dressage horse, Ilka just flowed across the ground, and whatever sort of rider was on her, she made that person feel like a million dollars. Her stable behavior was equally graceful and, unlike some of her pushier stable mates, her manners were impeccable.

Ilka's favorite companion was Rudyard, a white cat who adopted us and thereafter Ilka. The two became inseparable, and how lovely they looked strolling through the green pastures together. I still see so vividly in my mind the picture of her looking out from her dark stall, with Rudyard sitting so peacefully beside her. It is one of my most abiding and poignant memories.

It was Ilka who gave me the gift of one of those mystical moments that sometimes are granted to us humans. The two of us were out early one summer morning. The sky was that particular blue found only in Vermont. The earth sparkled with dew and fragile white cobwebs, laced like a quilt over the grass beside our track. Eventually, we emerged from the woods into a huge field. We started to trot, then glided into a lovely smooth canter.

I have never had any formal riding training, being more of a "just stay on if you can" sort of person, but suddenly I found myself standing straight up in the stirrups and, leaving the reins relaxed on Ilka's withers, I stretched out my arms to their fullest extent. Perfectly balanced, the two of us...well, there was no other word...we were flying, unattached to the solid earth. With Ilka's mane and tail streaming out into the breeze, the heavens high above, the soft turf below, the magical woods around us, we were one. One with each other and with the glorious mysteries around, above, and beneath us. A truly perfect moment. Perhaps it lasted thirty seconds, I don't remember. But it was perfection.

Thank you, Ilka, my beloved horse, for such an unexpected gift.

ANTICIPATION

Be Prepared

—Motto of both Girl Scouts and Boy Scouts of America

Lady-in-waiting (with young friend)

APRIL BROUGHT LAMBING SEASON, MY VERY FAVORITE TIME on the farm's calendar. Now, many years later, I still love to mull over my memories of that busy, bustling, creative month. If I had my life to do over again, I would have without hesitation chosen to be a midwife (of humans), so I suppose birthing lambs was in some measure a stand-in for that unfulfilled dream.

One late March day, several years into our sheep-farming career, my niece Elizabeth called me from Boston. Hugely pregnant at the time, she confided to me, "I've just had a wonderful weekend getting together the baby's things: layette, bassinet, toys, diapers. Everything's ready now." I laughed and told her she was "nesting" and that the baby would be sure to arrive very soon (it did, the very next day). When I put the telephone down and thought about my comment, I realized that nesting is precisely what I did myself just before lambing season.

For most of the year, Jim was, in the main, the one who took care of the flock—feeding and watering them morning and evening, letting them in and out from their grazing grounds, and repairing barn buildings and fencing. My normal purview was tending to our three horses and (of course) constantly doing the bidding of our numerous dogs. During lambing time, though, I spent every waking moment and a lot of half-awake moments up in the sheep pen, while Jim would take over stable duties if I was busy with a birth or waiting for one to happen.

Since the first due date for the ewes to start lambing was sometime during the first week of April, my nesting began about ten days before that D-day. For most of a day I disappeared into the cavernous sheep barn for hours to prepare for the new arrivals. First, I checked my lambing box, the shepherd's version of a doctor's black bag.[1] Into my box went scissors for trimming umbilical cords, iodine for dabbing on

---

[1] Do doctors use these anymore? I vividly remember my doctor grandfather's big black bag filled with all his medications and instruments. He never went anywhere, even to a rare night out at the theater, without it.

their raw ends, latex examination gloves, and lubricant to aid with deliveries. (Before I found out about commercial-size jars of lubricant sold in husbandry catalogues, I used K-Y jelly bought from our local CVS pharmacy. The number of tubes I purchased certainly tended to bring forth some strange looks from the person ringing up the sale!)

Next into the box went a length of baler twine. Sometimes during a delivery it was necessary to tie a loop around a lamb's emerging leg to keep it outside the mother and not let it pop back into the birth canal. To the twine, I added a couple of towels for wiping off newborns and a jar of antibiotic uterine boluses. These latter I used if I felt, especially after a complicated birth, that the mother might be in danger of an infection in her womb.

To complete this absolutely essential box, I washed a couple of baby bottles and nipples in case we had to put colostrum quickly into weak lambs. As a general rule, Scottish blackface lambs are very vigorous at birth because of the need to be mobile as soon as possible to escape predators, such as foxes (although there is, sadly, no escape in their native Scotland from that major predator, the beautiful golden eagle). But sometimes a newly born lamb might have difficulty recovering from the trauma of birth and be slow to get up and nurse from its mother. Then I would milk some colostrum from her, often with great difficulty if it was a restless and uncooperative ewe, and feed it to the lamb via a baby bottle with an enlarged hole in its nipple. I had observed that the mother ewes, while their babies were sucking, would nudge the baby's back near the tail to stimulate its sucking and I would try to simulate this same motion when feeding the bottle, often with success. As the thick, warm liquid slid slowly down into the cold stomach of the tiny baby, the result was always miraculous. Within five minutes, the lamb would be standing on its wobbly legs, hungrily fastened onto its mother's teats and sucking lustily.

Another of my pre-lambing tasks was to check that the old bureau we kept in the shearing room of the barn had an adequate supply of clean towels for wiping off the newborns. Also, in its top drawers I kept syringes and needles. I had found after our first lambing season that it was really necessary to know how to give medications by injection, either subcutaneous or intramuscular, and our veterinarian had taught (a very nervous) me how to give them in times of need. These medications (such as antibiotics, vitamin B, and electrolytes) for weakened mothers and a good painkiller were kept in a little refrigerator next to the bureau. The painkiller I found to be very effective if—and it was indeed a rare occasion, with our strongly maternal breed of sheep—a mother refused to let her new baby nurse. One of the reasons for such a refusal might be because she was in pain, and a good shot of analgesic would nearly always calm and relax her and usually solve the problem.

I also needed a bucket, soap, and a large thermos for warm water. Sometimes the lambs got a case of scours (diarrhea) and had to have their bottoms washed off. This was definitely one of my least favorite tasks but, nevertheless, needed to be done to keep the little creature clean until the anti-scours medicine kicked in.

I must mention here that if all these preparations make me sound like a veterinarian, nothing could be farther from the truth. I certainly did not in any way have enough experience for that title. Farming is a humbling business, and I learned very early on that when dealing with animals (especially sheep, who hide pain and sickness until nearly dead), the challenge was to know when I couldn't handle a situation and call an expert to help as quickly as possible.

My final job was to put together the lambing pens, or jugs, as they are called in the sheep world. These jugs consisted of small stalls made of three-foot-wide by five-foot-high wooden gates strapped together with—what else, but the farmer's faithful friend—baler twine! A couple of metal snap hooks were hung for water and grain buckets, and a plastic laundry basket was tied into a corner for hay. After a scattering of sweet lime to sanitize the earth floor, topped by a good mound of fresh hay to make a cozy nest for the babies, all was in readiness. Into these little enclosures, for about twelve hours, went the mothers and their newly born babies. This forced intimacy enabled the ewe to bond quickly with her lambs and gave Jim and me a chance to check that everything was well with them. For instance, we could ensure that the afterbirth had been expelled, the babies were feeding properly, and the mother was taking nourishment in the form of grain, hay, and warm water laced with molasses.

All contingencies prepared for as much as possible (there was, inevitably, some previously unthought-of emergency each year), I had one more important item to address. Down I drove to our village store to stock up on some human necessities—that is, food and drink (the latter much needed after an arduous birthing session). We then cancelled all appointments in our diary for the next three weeks and sat back to wait impatiently for the first birth of the season.

Tommy and Foxy, the mini horses, being groomed.

A Home for the Homeless

Jim and I were always suckers for anything hurt, abandoned, or otherwise in need of love and protection. We were to discover that this compassion was to act as a magnet for people who thought a farm was the perfect place to pass on (dump?) their unwanted or inconvenient animals. We therefore gave sanctuary to quite a variety of creatures.

One was a pygmy goat from neighbors who found caring for him too difficult. So did we. He turned out to be a real Houdini, finding his way under, over, and through anywhere we tried to contain him. He (like our sheep) particularly loved my rose garden. Luckily for us (and for him!), some visiting friends from Connecticut, whose ambition had always been to have a pet goat, popped the little fellow into their car and took him back home with them. Once again, my rose garden was saved from destruction.

Also off-loaded onto us was a pair of miniature horses, whom we trained to pull a little cart. But, like the goat, they loved to get out of the horse pastures and go visit neighbors—and even the village's general store once. Perhaps they hoped for a free ration of carrots. Eventually, they too were found a more suitable home with friends who had more time to look after them and trained them to drive in competitions.

Some other creatures, sadly, did not have such a happy ending. One day, six hens were left on our doorstep. But our chicken-farming career came and went very fast when these unfortunate birds fell prey to a fox shortly after their arrival and before we had had time to build a safe home for them. How careless we felt, but how difficult it always is to find any extra time on a busy farm for unexpected necessities, like a chicken coop and run.

And then there was the perennial question of The Pig. I have always loved pigs. They are the most intelligent of all domestic animals, and it had long been a cherished ambition of mine to have one for a companion. Jim was adamantly against the idea. "But," I would say earnestly, "swine are so clever and so clean. They can be toilet trained. We could even have it in the house with us. I'm sure the dogs wouldn't mind." I wasn't too sure about this latter statement, and it was certainly disproved when Bessie, sitting imperiously on Jim's knee in her usual position as Alpha Bitch (or should I amend that to Supreme Leader of All That Moves at Maple Avenue Farm), joined my husband in The Look. A totally negative, don't-even-continue-with-the-idea sort of look.

With a sigh, I would resign myself to another porkerless year. I was temporarily defeated, but maybe—just maybe—another day, another time.

Lambing Time

Your lamb shall be without blemish …

—The Holy Bible, "Book of Exodus"

Dinner time in the kitchen, Bessie supervising.

OF ALL THE EVENTS IN OUR FARMING YEAR, lambing was my favorite happening. I loved the daily challenges, the new life burgeoning in the barn, learning how to understand and best help the birthing process of each ewe, and the satisfaction that my Jim and I allowed ourselves after each day's successes. Even our failures taught us so much about how to avoid similar disappointments and tragedies in the future.

Every year on the first day of April, a date we reckoned that lambs might possibly start arriving, we started doing our nightly barn checks. Jim and I each had our "duty" hours; mine were at midnight and 6:00 a.m., Jim's at 3:00 a.m. We often met people who scoffed at the idea of disturbing their night's sleep just to check on "a few ol' sheep," but Jim and I believed that animals dependent on our care should be looked after responsibly. Why risk leaving a ewe in painful, troubled labor all night, perhaps to lose her and her offspring, because we were too lazy to leave our beds? And then, apart from the benefit of knowing that we were looking after our flock to the best of our ability, we benefited so much from these late night visits.

What beauty was to be found in the brilliant night skies, with occasionally a magical glimpse of the northern lights. If the moon was out and full, its luminescence would light up the landscape so we could see the whole valley spread out below us, punctuated by friendly lights from other farms' barns. In the deep silence, we could hear the sound of the little brook in full spate alongside the road below our farm; maybe an owl, hunting on its silent wings, would hoo-hoo-hoo from the pine forest, or a fox bark from its den near our pond.

Arriving at the barn, it would seem quiet at first until, gradually, the familiar, well-loved smells and sounds began to intrude on our sleepy senses. First to greet us was the dusty aroma of the old place, mixed with a faint overlay of manure, ammonia, and the sweet fragrance of rowen (the second cutting of the hay), which the sheep loved because of its tenderness. From various corners came the steady chomp-chomp sounds of the resting inhabitants chewing their cud or the tiny bleats of a lamb awaking to hunger pangs and being answered by a comforting low blaat from its dam. Sometimes I heard the long-drawn-out sigh of a prospective mother turning her huge bulk in search of a more comfortable position. I would feel such a surge of sympathy for this creature because, even so many years away from my own birthing experience, I still remembered that feeling of intense discomfort suffered at the very end of a pregnancy. Most important was to listen for the sound of a ewe's little whickering, which announced the arrival of a new lamb or two—even three! All these reasons made our nightly visits a truly treasured, unique, and unforgettable experience. And many times, when it was a cold, wet, or even snowy night, the return to a cozy bed and warm spouse seemed all the more delectable.

The first sign that a ewe was soon to give birth was a falling-in of her flanks, which heightened the prominence of her big belly and made it sag even farther toward the ground. After a couple of years in the lambing business we had developed an eye for this phenomenon, and it was the reason we sheared our ewes in March before they lambed. If they still had their thick winter coats, it would have been impossible to notice these really important signposts to an impending birth.

Within a day or two of this first change, the ewe would go off into a quiet corner alone and start pawing the ground. If we were around at this stage—and animals generally try very hard to make sure no human is around when they are giving birth—we would gently persuade her into one of the waiting jugs in the small room just off the barn's porch. Keeping these ready with clean bedding and a bucket of fresh water was one of our daytime chores. Once in this tiny enclosed space, we could deal with her delivery more easily should anything go amiss. Believe me, any shepherd's worst nightmare is the sight of a ewe running up the hillside with a lamb's head sticking out from her rear end, with little hope of catching her.

Within an hour or so of the pawing movements, contractions would start undulating through the ewe's body. As they came closer together, the water bag, which looks like a small balloon filled with dark-colored amniotic fluid, appeared from under her tail. Soon after this, if it was an uncomplicated birth, would follow a shiny black nose resting on two equally shiny and tiny black hooves. A few pushes by the ewe, and the little creature, covered in mucous, would slide swiftly out to land on the ground with a thud. Immediately the mother would turn around to welcome her baby, whickering quietly to it while she licked it clean. Sometimes I had to clear the nose and mouth of mucous and rub the baby vigorously if it seemed unresponsive, but mostly, after an initial sneeze or two, the newborn would be staggering to its feet within minutes and searching for milk—really, the most miraculous moment.

Taking great care not to alarm the new mother by over-handling her precious baby, I would gently trim the straggling umbilical cord to about two inches long and dip it in iodine. I also "stripped" the ewe's teats to make sure the colostrum was flowing, as sometimes after birth the nipple would be blocked by a waxy plug. Stripping requires a slightly firmer downward motion on the teat than that employed for regular milking. It also definitely needs good warm hands; any self-respecting animal will swiftly withhold her largesse if touched by freezing digits! Finally, after giving the tired mother a little grain and filling her bucket with warm water mixed with molasses to boost her energy, the new family was left in peace to get to know each other.

If there were a lot of ewes producing offspring at the same time, life became a bit chaotic. We once had a writer friend staying with us, and although she was the kindest of people and very anxious to help with our labors in the barn, her knowledge of shepherding was nil. One afternoon she happened to arrive at the scene of a particularly fraught moment. A ewe was just birthing in one corner. A couple of other new babies and mothers had become separated from each other and were frantically milling around, all bleating at the top of their voices. I was struggling to stop one of our giddier ewes, her afterbirth not yet released from her uterus and trailing behind her on the floor, from heading out the door. Our friend came running over to help me, only to be stopped dead in her tracks as I shrieked at her, "Don't tread on the afterbirth!" In her haste to be of use, she hadn't noticed that this rather gruesome-looking bag of tissue was still attached to its owner and she didn't know that it was very dangerous to detach one from the other precipitately. Poor woman—she nearly leapt through the roof in alarm. Thereafter, she quickly came to the conclusion that she could be more supportive of us by staying down in the safety of the house, working quietly on her novel and cooking supper for us each night.

While the majority of our ewes had strong, sturdy offspring with no trouble, sometimes a lamb (or lambs) was wrongly positioned in the uterus or in the birth canal and could not be birthed without help. This kind of trouble signaled itself when the water bag had been passed but, after half an hour or so, was not followed by the sight of an emerging head. Or sometimes, only the head appeared with no accompanying feet. Or yet again, we might not see a head but only two feet. Then it became time to take a hand in the situation (a very apt metaphor, as you will see).

With Jim holding the straining mother's head, I would don a rubber glove, pour a liberal amount of lubrication into my palm, and slowly put my hand into the ewe's vagina. It constantly amazed and humbled me that however much the ewe might be struggling to get away from her handlers, the moment I entered her body she calmed right down, as if she knew that I was going to help her with her pain and discomfort. After a gentle internal search, I'd maybe find the problem was a simple one, such as a front leg curved back instead of forward, which made it impossible for the baby to progress through the cervix. All I had to do was carefully hook a finger behind the tiny knee and ease it into the birth canal parallel with the other leg so that the mother could deliver without difficulty. That was an easy scenario.

A "hands-in" investigation!

There were many more complicated ones, as, for instance, twins fighting for who should leave first; triplets completely mixed up, with no room to move them around into birthing positions; a lamb with a really large head, which made it extremely difficult for the mother to push it out. There were even occasions when it was hard for me to work out whether I was feeling a rump or a neck, a back or a front leg—or maybe a tail? Almost always I was able to work things out, and although I hated to give up, I never forgot one of our farm's mantras: if in doubt, call the vet. And how blessed we were to be served by a first-class veterinarian practice of three highly skilled women, not to mention our local horse doctor who so willingly came when called in an immediate emergency.

Birthing the big-headed lambs was my least favorite task, and with our breed of sheep the ram lambs' heads were larger than normal because of their horn buds. It was very painful for both the mother and me. I had to reach through the cervix, cup the lamb's head in my hand, and gently try to pull it into the daylight. The cervix and the head both felt rock hard, and my poor hand played pig in the middle. After a couple of these deliveries, I had a hand that looked as though I'd been practicing lightweight boxing!

Sometimes for these big-head deliveries I would have to get the baby out by tying baler twine around its two protruding front legs and pulling, a process that needed a surprising amount of strength. I tried to use this latter method only as a last resort, since when such strong suction was exerted to get the lamb out it sometimes could result in the mother having a uterine prolapse. This is a condition whereby the ewe expels not only the baby but her whole uterus as well. When this happened, we had to call in the veterinarian. She had to push the uterus back inside into its normal position—no easy task, as a sheep's womb is about the size and consistency of a large balloon, only far more rubbery and slippery. The vagina was then stitched shut for a week or so to prevent the ewe repeating the expulsion process during her postpartum contractions.

Every lambing season we seemed to meet with one or two new problems, and it was a source of endless comfort to me to have Jim at the other end of the ewe giving me the confidence not to panic but to calmly and patiently work through the problem. And when things were at last accomplished safely, how fantastically satisfying it was to sit back in bloody and exhausted triumph and watch the new lamb, although a little shaky after such a rough journey into its new world, rise at last onto its bendy legs and bravely start searching for milk, that life-sustaining liquid. The proud mother, also bloody and exhausted but so touchingly proud, would gently help her baby by nudging it in the direction of her udder.

Birthings didn't always work out well. Over our nearly twenty years of lambing seasons, there were certainly a few unforgettable hours of bloody toil that resulted in bringing forth a dead lamb or a mother that needed to be euthanized. Over and over we learnt the same bitter lesson that farming deals not only with life but often also with death. We tried to learn to take the sad times with equanimity, but it was hard because we were so fond of all our sheep and knew intimately all their varied personalities.

It was not an easy path the two of us had chosen to tread, but even with the bumps and potholes along the way we would not have wanted in any way to end our journey.

Maternal pride

The Diary

During lambing time we kept a notebook on the kitchen counter and, upon returning from the barn, we would write messages in it to each other about any goings-on in the barn. Many of these messages were in our own kind of shorthand and not understandable to anyone else. Here are a few of our more legible (and censored) samples:

April 5, 6:00 a.m. [Roz] Puffball had big ewe lamb, both legs back. Got it out. Poor Puffy, very tired but so happy and proud. Lamb v. strong. Sleep well my love. Pearly. [Jim's nickname for me]

April 6, midnight [Roz] Goldie Horn twins—R and E. Very noisy. Slow to find nipples so bottled each 2 ccs. My love, P.

April 8, 2:00 a.m. [Jim] Dogs in a great state, raccoon must be out and about. No movement of any sort in barn. Love you, J.

April 9, midnight [Roz] Moon so bright I didn't need a flashlight. Stream sounds like the Niagara Falls. No action but *very* loud breathing from four *very* large ladies-in-waiting. Should we start a musical quartet called The Grunts? Sleep well, my love.

April 9, 3:00 a.m. [Jim] Cloudless, moon a perfect circle. Watch Emerald! You are my light, Pearly. J.

April 9, 6:00 a.m. [Roz] Emerald—two ewe lambs! Born outside in pouring rain. Noisiest two I've ever heard. Poor Em in a bit of a tizzy with all the yelling so gave her a shot of Banamine to calm her down. Ramadan's first progeny, we must congratulate him later! Tell Onyx to get a move on…I'm tired. Love R.

April 11, 9:00 p.m. [Jim] Ruby—2 ram lambs— doesn't seem too happy with them. Check. Where is the flashlight? J.

April 11, midnight [Roz] Ruby seems to have rejected one lamb; he is very cold so I brought him down to the kitchen to warm him up and gave him a bottle. Bessie immediately climbed into his basket and started to lick him all over which was a perfect way to revive him. Have left another bottle for you to give him. Sleep well.

April 11, 3:00 a.m. [Jim] Kitchen lamb doing well, thanks to Bessie's ministrations; will try returning him to Ruby but he may remain a bottle baby.

April 12, 3:00 a.m. [Jim] Cold, windy, rainy, a night not fit for man or beast. Obviously the girls think so too, absolutely zip happening. Coyote howled from the woods. Love you, my Pearly.

April 12, 6:00 a.m. [Roz] Found Charlotte with 2 ewe lambs. All doing well. Had to stop and admire Goldie Horn's twins, she is very proud of them. My love, R.

...7:30 a.m. Flora MacDonald—2 ewe lambs, one very large, one very small. Tubed the little one. Then Roz had a very difficult time delivering triplets from Foxglove. Took an hour but finally got them all sorted out and birthed. Everyone exhausted, but the babies all healthy and sucking. Lots of molasses water for Foxglove and a shot of Vit. B to perk her up tea with a slug of brandy for Roz.

"*Who are you?*"

...11:00 a.m. Diwali also had triplets. Virginia yelling for a lost baby, found it under the hayrack. Think Mona Lisa in labor, could be difficult. All hell breaking loose. When did I last eat! Xxxxxx

April 13, 4:30 a.m. [Jim] Phoebe had lamb and then prolapsed. Jadine [our vet] came and pushed it all back and sewed it in. Stitches out in a few days. Mother is resting quietly and lamb okay. Whew, what a night!

April 17, 3:25 a.m. [Annie, my sister-in-law who came to help us by doing a couple of night duties] Ohhh, Roz, what a marvelous experience that was! All was quiet, girls standing around on porch and two in birthing room. Manny drank down his bottle happily once I was able to position him and the flashlight; couldn't find his mouth at first! Virginia seems much more alert. The night is so beautiful and star filled, loved the sound of the running river too. Almost wanted to go for a walk. Thanks for letting me be a part of this pulsing life. Lay awake a long time anticipating it so I'll sleep in a bit. Love, Annie.

And these were just moderately peaceful days and nights!

WE WERE AS TWINN'D LAMBS THAT DID FRISK I' THE SUN, AND BLEAT THE ONE AT THE OTHER

—William Shakespeare (*The Winter's Tale*)

Hollyhock enjoying having her babies admired

THERE WAS PLENTY OF OTHER WORK TO DO IN THE SPARE MOMENTS when lambs were not being born. Within twelve hours of their birth, we needed to give each lamb an ear tag and dock its tail—what Jim and I called "topping and tailing." The former was essential because our flock was registered with the Scottish Blackface Association and therefore every animal we bred was required to have a number for identification. Tail docking was necessary for a hygienic reason. This grisly task was definitely not my favorite occupation, and many times I would wonder if we really needed to do it. And then I'd remember the hot summer days to come, when maggots under a long tail can become a most disgusting problem to deal with. These little fat white worms feast on the delicate and vulnerable areas of skin around a sheep's anus or vulva, causing intense irritation, soreness, and sometimes infection.

To perform the docking operation, we used an electric tool called a Burdizzo castrator. (It also could be used to neuter ram lambs, but that's something we generally did not do.) It looked rather like a heavy pair of shears. The cutting blade was heated to a high temperature so that the tail was simultaneously cut off and the raw end cauterized; we very rarely had any ensuing infections. Jim would hold the little victim as I worked the tool, trying to comfort myself with the knowledge that this tiny bit of fleshy tail had very limited nerve development at that early stage of the lamb's life. In fact, although the poor little creature did struggle a little during the process, as soon as it was returned to its (highly indignant) mother and had had a good comforting slurp from her udder, it never seemed to show any further pain or even discomfort.

Also at this topping-and-tailing time we gave the mother a quick checkup. We had a special chair, which looked rather like those old-fashioned canvas deck chairs. The ewe was gently backed up to the chair and tipped into it in a sitting position. Her movements then being very limited, I was able to trim her hooves, give her an injection of vitamin B and selenium (there is not enough selenium in our local Vermont soil, and lack of it can lead to brittle bones in animals), and, finally, to feel her udder for any signs of mastitis. All being well, mother and child were returned to their jug to recover from the indignities inflicted upon them both.

The day after all this postpartum work, the little family would be moved out of their tiny jug and into a bigger room on the sunny side of the barn, which had a small outside area surrounded by an old stone wall. This we called the nursery, and here they stayed for a week. The nervous new mothers carefully stashed their babies away in dark corners, under the hay feeders, in openings of the stone wall, or under the barn steps—anywhere to keep them safely out of sight. When I visited the barn, I would come across little hidden heaps of black and white bodies carefully guarded by their fierce mothers, who stamped their forelegs in warning if I approached too near.

As these engaging little creatures started to gain strength, it was such fun to watch them practicing little hops and skips. Then they started to play games, such as king of the castle or hide-and-seek on and around the manure pile, while the ram lambs butted heads in imitation of their grown-up sires.

After a week in the small space of the nursery, each ewe and her offspring were moved over to the main pen. It was a sort of merry-go-round as the ewe originated in the main pen, then had her baby and went into a jug, from there into the nursery, and thence back to where she had started. After this final move, there was a great deal of comparing each other's children by the mothers (seemingly accompanied by—judging from the noise—quite a few derogatory comments) and touching, sniffing, and head butting between the lambs. Added to all these goings-on were the loud sighs of exhaustion from the very large mothers-in-waiting as their favorite resting places were commandeered by yet another gang of newcomers.

Now that the babies were in a larger space with more room to run around, the very best game of all could take place. Jim and I called this "the running of the lambs." It took place morning and evening during feeding time. While Scotties are excellent mothers, very protective and strict with their progeny, when feeding time arrived, even the best of those mothers forgot their babies in the mad rush to swallow as much grain as possible in the shortest time. Their lambs, temporarily released from their mothers' eagle eyes, then gathered in an unruly bunch at one end of the collapsed foundation wall of an old pigsty and at some unseen signal went running, rushing, and swooping with joy along it, leaping and pronging (jumping in the air with all four legs stiff) and dancing to the far end, there to gather in a gang again before repeating the whole game in the other direction. This enchanting performance went on until it was promptly ended

The running of the lambs

by peremptory bleats from anxious dams now finished with supper and wanting to take control over their errant children again.

The exception to those youngsters running along the wall were the "bummers." Each year, there was always a lamb or two rejected by its mother. Maybe it had been a hard birth and the mother was too tired to bond well. Maybe she had twins or triplets and one got neglected. Or sometimes a lamb might be born with extra sharp teeth and (understandably) his dam didn't like him suckling her. Whatever the reason, evening feeding time was the bummers' Moment of Opportunity. While the ewes' heads were sunk deep into the feeding troughs, they would race along the line of udders so conveniently on display and take a quick swig from as many teats, no matter whose, as possible. Poor bummers—they were a sad, raggedy-tag lot, but survivors all. When weaning time came, they didn't have the same parting pangs as their more-loved siblings and soon fattened up on the sweet spring grass.

And so the work went on until the last lamb had finally arrived, the last mother and baby had been treated, and a full night's sleep much appreciated. It was time to move everyone from the now rather cramped main pen and put them all into the big pasture below our house. Here there was plenty of tasty spring grazing and, for the little ones, acres of space to run around and strengthen their muscles.

Production over for another year, I would sadly dismantle my lambing box and clean out the pens. Both Jim and I would be very tired, but what a thrill it was to stand in our garden and look down on the beauty of our enlarged flock. As Jim remarked each year, "Well, Pearly, my love, we knew less than nothing about sheep or farming when we arrived here, and now look at what we've achieved. I'm proud of us!"

After an intense few weeks, when my whole being had been concentrated on the fecundity of the sheep-fold, I would feel quite withdrawn from the real world. Somewhat reluctantly, I'd acknowledge that it was time once again to take up the reins of normal living. The garden was full of weeds; my horse had grown too fat from lack of exercise; dogs, family, and friends were feeling neglected. Then I'd hear those charming words of Robert Frost echo through my mind:

> *Ah, when to the heart of man*
> *Was it ever less than a treason*
> *To go with the drift of things,*
> *To yield with a grace to reason,*
> *And bow and accept the end*
> *Of a love or a season?*
> (from "Reluctance")

Churchill's Triumph

One year, local flocks were being attacked repeatedly by coyotes. Although we always brought our sheep into the main strongly fenced pen at night, we were still worried about our herd's vulnerability during the day, especially when their lambs were small. Although our llama, Lloyd, grazed with them—and we knew that shepherds out west sometimes used these camelids as guard animals—somehow we couldn't imagine our lackadaisical llama trying to defend anything, especially the sheep whom, like everyone else, animal or human, he appeared to despise.

Churchill conversing with a ram friend

So after some research, we decided to purchase a guard dog who would live with the sheep and defend them from all dangers. The beguiling puppy we brought home was of the Maremma breed, used by Italian mountain shepherds. He was large and floppy, with pure white shaggy hair. What to call him? We thought at once of Great Britain's WWII prime minister, Winston Churchill, and his stirring speeches about fighting on the beaches and in the fields. And so the pup became known as Churchill.

What a sweet-natured little fellow he turned out to be, who always greeted us with smiling ecstasy. It became harder and harder to leave him alone with "his" sheep, who actually bullied him, and to feel his wistful eyes following us back to the farmhouse.

Lambing over, the flock (with the unwilling dog amongst them) was quartered in the field surrounding the house. Churchill would sit and gaze into the kitchen window all day. Our children sniggered to each other over the telephone and had a sweepstakes going as to how long Jim and I would be able to hold out before Churchill became a house dog.

Time passed, and winter descended upon us. The pressure increased until, finally, we relented somewhat (family betting was raised). Churchill was to be allowed in during the day but had to go out at night when predators were more likely to strike. He started to look smug; he had a paw in the door. This system worked quite well for a while except that come bedtime, Jim would slink quietly upstairs and I would be left to put an increasingly unwilling dog out into the cold darkness.

Then came the night when the wind was roaring and the rain was positively deluging down. The sheep were snug in the barn, but I knew Churchill wouldn't join them. Dog and I stood there looking at each other. A minute later my husband, snugly tucked up in bed with our two other dogs, was startled by the appearance in the doorway of wife and Maremma. Firmly I announced that if he wanted Churchill to go out on a night like this, he would have to do it himself this time. The battle was over, won paws down by canine passive resistance. Thenceforth, Churchill performed his guarding duties while blissfully asleep at Jim's bedside.

My only concern about this new arrangement was the thought that should the winter temperatures fall far below zero, Churchill might consider it a three-dog night and feel it incumbent upon himself to keep us extra warm by joining us, Bessie, and Agnes on—or in—our bed. I had the worrisome feeling that in this event, I might be the one sleeping on the floor.

What's in a Name?

Holla your name to the reverberate hills …

—William Shakespeare (*Twelfth Night*)

The infamous William Wallace!

SHAKESPEARE, AS SO OFTEN WITH THIS FAMOUS WRITER, turned out to be dead right in this bit of advice. It was certainly followed on Maple Avenue Farm. Jim and I had a habit of giving names to everything, including our different pastures and some of the machinery, as well as our animals. We liked to imagine that by taking so much trouble naming all our beloved creatures, we were providing an intimacy and affection for them that expressed our all-encompassing compassion for the animal kingdom, both wild and domesticated.

Of course, the sheep never doubted they were on the front line of this distinction. I'm sure our other animals felt the same way, but, unlike the constant blatting of their ovine neighbors, they didn't make quite so much noise about it. Undoubtedly, our neighbors near and far (who often suffered through noisy sheep roundups) would agree with the truth of Shakespeare's words. I don't think there was ever any doubt that everyone on our sunny hillside did indeed holla their names—from the famous to the fabulous—to the reverberate hills.

We had First Ladies, just like the White House. Ours had arrived at the start of our first summer at the farm and, in true Scottish blackface tradition, had demanded an individual identity almost immediately after being unloaded from our truck. It was at that time that we came up with the idea of using a different theme each year, which would immediately tell us how old the animal was. So for these forerunners of our sheep production line, family and friends were chosen as our motif. My mother, Sheila; Jim's two sisters, Marcia and Macy; and a close friend, Barbara, were honored by having the four little ewes called after them. The one ram lamb, because of his rather earnest look and curly hair, was christened Bernie after our then-mayor of Burlington, Vermont, Bernie Sanders.

Subsequent years saw the appearance of flower sheep: Daffodil, Hollyhock, Foxglove, and beautiful Magnolia, a Southern belle we imported from Virginia. Then we used rivers: Mississippi, Shenandoah, and Ravi the Ram (named after a river in northwestern India and northeastern Pakistan). Another year, bursting upon this earthly scene came Venus and Diana and the heavenly twins, Ariel and Titania, with Pluto as their handsome consort. At times, the names of such famous personages as Susan B. Anthony, Flora Mac-Donald, Cleopatra, and Pocahontas were heard echoing across the valley.

The year of gems produced a very special little ram lamb, Zircon, who had a twin sister, called Sapphire. These two became orphans at birth when their mother died of a uterine hemorrhage. We reared them on bottles and they grew apace and were very devoted to each other—inseparable, in fact. One day, when Jim went to check that all was well in the sheep pen, Zircon came running down from the hillside bleating and appearing very distressed. He continued to cry to Jim, and since there was no sign of Sapphire, Jim realized that Zircon was trying to convey that something was wrong. Upon searching, Jim found the little ewe lamb huddled against a stone wall in great distress from bloat, a common and difficult-to-prevent stomach condition that can happen with bottle-fed babies.

Sadly, it was too late to save her, but we were so impressed by the intelligence and brotherly love Zircon had shown that we felt he deserved an honored place on our farm. Unfortunately, as he didn't have the looks to become a breeding ram, the only way he could be kept was to run him with the ewes. But as we didn't want him to mate with them, we went against our usual policy and had him castrated. On the flip side, Zircon lived with us for many years as a chubby, cheerful, and beloved wether, who became a really calming influence as a leader of the often flighty female members of the flock.

While on the subject of wethers, I have to include this story about another wether (at least, a sort of one, as you will see). This tale is about a ram we called William Wallace, of *Braveheart* fame, named in our year of fictional heroes. He—the ram, not the hero—was the son of Hollyhock. WW was such an exceptionally handsome yearling, with long, thick fleece that touched the floor, that Jim decided to take him to the Maryland Sheep and Wool Festival, which he attended every May with the best specimens from our flock. The great moment came when proud shepherd and exhibition ram strode into the ring. The judge (as with most judges we came across) didn't know much about Scottish blackface sheep or that WW was really a pussycat with beautiful manners and was nervous of our ram's enormous bulk and very lethal looking horns.

Therefore, this nervous man neglected to examine this particular competitor closely. But he was so impressed with William that he awarded him a purple ribbon! Jim was thrilled with their success and stood outside the prizewinners' pen for the rest of the day, proudly accepting accolades from other breeders and show visitors.

Stand off!

Next day, there was a shearing exhibition taking place, and Jim decided to have WW shorn of his thick winter coat in preparation for the hot weather to come. The shearer went to work. A little while later he came to an abrupt halt. "I don't believe it!" he shouted. A host of onlookers craned their necks to see what the excitement was about. The shearer straightened up and looking at Jim incredulously—and, unfortunately, in a very carrying voice—uttered the eternally damning words, "This ram's got no balls!"

What a calamity to fall on a shepherd of repute, who hadn't noticed this lack either—and neither had his wife. The real truth of the matter was that William did have testicles, they just had not descended (a condition that can be found in both man and beast). Poor William was quietly loaded onto our truck and driven home. As he was such a sweet-natured animal, but obviously of no use to our flock, we found him a loving home as a companion to a donkey.

Now, back to the business in hand: cognomens. After several years, and as our Scottie flock multiplied, we also fell in love with another breed—Black Welsh Mountain sheep. Taking a few rare days off, we drove down to Maryland to a very beautiful riverside estate, complete with an old Southern mansion. Here we purchased three ewe lambs and one very handsome year-old ram. As well as so liking these attractive little blackish brown animals, we had another reason for introducing them to our farm. In Australia and New Zealand, black sheep provide a good way of counting very large flocks. The shepherd puts in one black sheep to every ten white sheep and then knows roughly the size of his herd by counting only the black ones. So, since that year we had enlarged our flock to thirty, we added our three new black ones. They were christened Rosa Parks, Maya Angelou, and Diana Ross. The ram—obviously kept separately in the ram field—we called Cadwgan (pronounced "ca-du-gan"), after the previous owner of our farm, a true Welsh name indeed.

Unfortunately, and very typically, our Scottish flock hated the Welsh girls and refused to have anything to do with them. Jim and I wondered whether this was due to the eons-old antipathy between two Celtic nationalities.

Over the following years, what laughs we had as we went from film stars (Marilyn Monroe, Judi Dench, Elizabeth Taylor) to fictional characters (Scarlett O'Hara, Anna Karenina, Lorna Doone) to international festivals. I particularly liked the spiritual names we picked one year, for who could resist rams named Baa Mitzvah, Ramadan, or Ullambana?

It was during this year of festivals that, needing some new bloodlines for the flock, we drove into New York State, way down past the Finger Lakes to the Mount Saviour Monastery. Here, the resident monks had been breeding Scottish blackface for many years and had a large flock for us to choose from. Triumphantly, we returned home with two lambs—one male, whom we named (very appropriately, we thought) Ascension, and a rather weedy-looking ewe lamb. Her appearance was not much to shout about but her bloodlines were excellent, and we knew that a few months on good green pasture would fill out her meager frame and put a bounce in her (at that time) droopy posture. She, we called Assumption.

Ascension turned out to be very aptly named in that he became not only a very efficient sire but also a shepherd's nightmare: a "fence jumper." Soon after his September arrival, and therefore a short while before our formal Tupping (mating) Day, this young ram jumped into the ewes' field one dark night and bred the one sheep he was familiar with—tiny Assumption. Then, obviously scared of being punished for this dastardly deed, he jumped back into his own pasture, where he assumed a pose of complete innocence. Jim and I therefore spent the following winter in blissful ignorance of poor Assumption's early deflowering, and it was not until early one March morning that the results of Ascension's little peccadillo became obvious. Out in a far corner of the snowy sheep pen was Assumption, now the mother of a tiny, but nonetheless very strong, ewe lamb. Since we had no idea—at that time, anyway—from whose loins this little stranger had sprung, obviously there was only one name we could give this surprise arrival. She became known as, who else, but Immaculate Conception! The mystery of IC's paternity was eventually solved when Ascension was caught red-hoofed in a repeat raid into the ewes' pasture the following October.

And then there were the golden oldie songs. We really loved this year. Joining us after lambing were Moon River, Tea for Two (T.T.), and Unforgettable, who turned out to be most aptly named as she became one of the most ornery sheep we ever bred. A very favorite ram of ours (particularly of my Jim's, whose pride and joy this animal was from birth onwards) we called Only Ewe. As a mature ram, he won Best of Breed at the Maryland Sheep and Wool Festival. This was quite an achievement as he was up against stiff competition from other, better-known breeds. Only Ewe had the sweetest nature and would let children ride on his massive, wooly back while holding onto his huge, curved horns. Our champion's portrait graces Page 2 of this book and the original hangs to this day in my kitchen, where it is much admired.

Of course, such an exotic bunch of names tended to be a little confusing to guests staying with us or dropping by for tea or coffee, most of them, poor things, already bewildered enough by what they saw as our very crazy and peculiar lifestyle. I remember a particularly funny incident that happened one November. While up in the pens tupping was in full swing, I was sitting over a cup of tea in the kitchen with a group of friends. Enter Jim, who announced casually to us all that he'd just seen Rhett Butler tupping Emerald, that General Montcalm and Lucille Ball were really going strong together, and that, unfortunately, Cleopatra didn't seem to find Ramadan very attractive. Not to mention that Denzel Washington was fighting again with Baa Mitzvah. Poor bewildered friends, indeed.

*   *   *   *   *

Lloyd proudly posing.

Although not ovine related (and we did have other animals of great character living with us, they just took a bit of a backseat most of the time), I couldn't finish this chapter on names without mentioning a very unique animal who lived with us on the farm: our llama. Jim had always wanted to own a llama, not for any particular reason other than he just wanted to have one. Shortly after we started shepherding, we made inquiries of local llama breeders as to what they had on the market. One small farm we contacted was badly in need of an affectionate home for an orphaned, five-month-old, bottle-fed baby. So anxious were they for us to have him that they offered to deliver him to us.

A few days later their small truck ground its way up our steep hill. On the front seat of their truck, kneeling between them, was this odd-looking small brown animal. With nose pointing in a distinctly upward angle, his huge brown eyes viewed his new world and us in a distinctly disdainful way. He looked so regal I was reminded of the king of England and almost expected him to raise a small hoof in that slow wave so well known to royalty watchers. Jim and I felt a bit uncomfortable in our usual scruffy farm attire and wished we had dressed a little more formally for this grand arrival.

Our new little camelid's behavior patterns were anything but regal, however, and a great deal of spitting and swearing issued forth from this latest addition to the Maple Avenue Farm family. So royal names were definitely not to be considered. What to call him? After much input from family and friends far and wide (and much sprightly leaping out of the way of well-aimed saliva), we settled on the only truly suitable name for him: Lloyd. Lloyd the Llama lived with us for many years.

As he grew from babyhood, Lloyd did not in actuality become what one would call a good-looking specimen of llamahood. Perhaps in modern parlance he would be labeled "aesthetically challenged." His ears never grew more than an inch tall (he was born far out in a pasture on a snowy night, so we think they were frostbitten), his legs were terribly bandy, and his teeth would be a dream come true for any orthodontist. Personality-wise, he was also a rather moody animal, a trait I realize now probably had a lot to do with the fact that we didn't know very much about llama characteristics and also that, at least for his first years with us, poor Lloyd was a classically misunderstood and frustrated teenager.

We had hoped that the company of a female llama might mute Lloyd's eccentricities and make him a happier, more tractable animal. We even started to make inquiries about a wife for him. She would have been called, of course, Dolly Llama. However, much to our dismay, in late adolescence Lloyd became troubled with an overabundance of male hormones. One afternoon, there was an embarrassing incident involving an elderly (and, unfortunately, rather prudish) lady friend of ours being jumped from behind and pushed over by an over-exuberant Lloyd. He, even with no parents to instruct him on the subject of camelid sex, must have instinctively known that llamas make love lying down. We quickly rescued our fallen friend, dusted her off, apologized profusely, and never told her what a narrow escape she had had.

Obviously, Lloyd really needed a wife. Desperately, we upped our search for a suitable female but, regrettably, in the end she just proved too expensive a purchase for us. We were, after all, sheep farmers; there was to be no folly such as a Dolly for Lloyd. The reluctant decision was made to call in the veterinarian, and Lloyd's life from then on was as a ball-less bachelor—or, in deference to his South American ancestry, a *soltero sin cojones*.

And he never did get any easier to live with.

Fourth of July Parade

Lloyd and the Fourth of July Parade

Here's another Lloyd story, one that is still remembered many years later by those who witnessed the scene.

On the whole, Lloyd led a very placid life. However, the one exception was on the Fourth of July, when he took part in the village parade. How he loved his hour of glory marching round the town green with Jim in tow, all the while being cheered on by the crowd of onlookers. Over the years he became a much-loved community Parade Personality. Lloyd was also much admired, if not always appreciated, for his unerring aim with his saliva.

One parade day, Lloyd, while passing in front of a house, was harassed by a particularly obnoxious Jack Russell terrier—the very same Beaver who had been Agnes's would-be suitor. Beaver barked and yipped at poor Lloyd while trying to snap at his heels. The first time this happened, Lloyd ignored the situation with his often-used expression of lofty hauteur.

The second time the parade rolled past the terrier's house, however, and the same performance started up again, Lloyd came to a dignified halt. Watched with great anticipation by a curious audience, he made a few strange gurgling sounds and some peculiar mouth movements. Then, to the accompaniment of loud claps and cheers, he spat out a huge green gob of spit, which arced through the air and landed bang slap in the middle of Beaver's face.

With a yelp of surprise and outrage, poor Beaver rushed inside his house, not to emerge until hours later, a chastened but—being a Jack Russell—inevitably unrepentant canine. Lloyd, meanwhile, with the faintest of nods acknowledging his loyal (lloyal?) fans, proceeded on his triumphant march.

Ever Hear of a Bankrupt Worm?

Worm: kinds of invertebrate limbless creeping animal,

some of which are parasitic in the intestines

—Oxford English Dictionary

Parasite: an animal or plant living in, with, or on

another organism

—Oxford English Dictionary

WHILE I AM SURE THAT THE HEADING OF THIS CHAPTER will not inspire any particularly warm feelings in my readers, the fact of the matter is that parasites, or the constant fight against them, are a very important part of husbandry, as any good, caring livestock owner will tell you. And since this is a book on farming—of both its charms and the nitty-gritty parts—the trials and tribulations of de-worming have to be included.

There are many kinds of parasites that can lurk in or on a sheep, and the bankrupt ones most probably in or on Wall Street too, but this chapter is about ovine, not human, predators. (A warning to readers here: you might like to take a deep breath before going over the following list.) On the internal front, sheep have to fight not only with the aforesaid bankrupt worms, but also with lungworms, tapeworms, roundworms, threadworms, nodular worms, large-mouth bowel worms, brown stomach worms, barber's pole worms, screwworms, whipworms, meningeal worms, liver flukes, and nose bots. Externally, sheep can be hosts to ticks, wool maggots, lice, and the common scab mite. (No one ever seemed able to tell me if there is an uncommon scab mite, so let's hope there isn't one.)

The ewes could not be wormed during pregnancy, so it was not until the beginning of May, when lambing was finally over, that Jim and I got ourselves organized for the great Operation Parasite Begone. While science might describe this operation in such technical terms as "the elimination of parasites from the intestinal track of ovines," Jim and I simply talked about worming, or drenching, the sheep. To unwary friends, especially those from the city, this all sounded a little dubious. And much to our amusement, they invariably thought worming had something to do with the rear end, rather than the head end, of a sheep (although, to be fair to them, they were partly right since the parasites are eliminated via the rear end).

At the beginning of our career as shepherds, Jim and I read and digested information about parasite removal from our various sheep manuals. These books recommended ordering something called a drencher, which, upon arrival, turned out to look like a gun with a long thin nozzle. The nozzle was attached by a long tube to a large plastic bottle full of the worming medication, a thick, white liquid. Then this whole contraption was strapped across the operator's chest. The gun nozzle was inserted into the sheep's mouth, the trigger squeezed, and the dose squirted down the throat of the reluctant victim. The trouble with this technique was that while in theory it all sounded very easy, in practice it never seemed to work very well. The nozzle frequently would get jammed or the tube from the bottle would come off, and Jim, the sheep, and I ended up in total frustration. So, as often happened, we threw out the official way of doing things and opted for our own, much simpler modus operandi.

Operation Parasite Begone (or OPB) unfolded in several stages. Stage one was undertaken by me in the kitchen. I filled small individual plastic syringes with 4cc's of the worming medication and put them all (with extra doses to replace those that went wide of the mark), along with a can of red spray paint, into a bucket.

Meanwhile, Jim was up by the sheep pen working on stage two: the rounding up and penning in of the female flock—not an easy task. The ewes, extra skittish because of the presence of their young lambs, had to be persuaded that the banging of the feed bucket betokened a bonus feeding and not anything more sinister. Anyone who calls sheep stupid didn't know our girls. They were well aware there was a chance that being called up from the pastures at a different dinnertime might mean Something Nasty was afoot. But greed usually superseded suspicion. Therefore, once they had all thundered into the pen, with much frantic bleating of lambs and loud return yells from their mothers, Jim had to be very spry about shutting the gate before they realized this operation was all a big con because, in the blink of an eye, the whole flock could turn around and barge right out again.

During this stage, I had to keep completely out of sight. To our ewes, I was the person who administered inoculations and medications and, no doubt, was known amongst them as Her with the Needle. It would have been a disaster if they had glimpsed me (or even my shadow) approaching in what I called my "Ter-

Operation Parasite Begone!

minator" outfit—padded overalls, heavy boots, bucket of syringes in one hand, spray paint in the other—before Jim had them safely shut in the small pen. Even the slightest suspicion by one ewe that something untoward was happening and within two seconds every sheep, however old, decrepit, or lame, would have vanished into the wide yonder of our very bottom pasture and days would have elapsed before they would think of approaching the pen again.

We eventually proceeded to stage three. Since the ewes were the most difficult part of the flock to work with, we tackled them first while our energy level was high. They were already cross at being packed into a tight space, and cooperation was definitely not on their minds. This made it a very difficult task, even for the deftest hands, to put a small plastic syringe into a ewe's mouth and push the plunger. While poor Jim struggled gamely to hold her still, each ewe, probably certain her last hour had come, would writhe and twist, clamp her mouth firmly shut, or hang her head to the ground. Her neighbors, meanwhile, would be shoving me from the rear or treading on my feet (giving me the usual painful case of "wormer's foot"), all of which might cause me to miss my target entirely and squirt the medication all over myself, Jim, and various wooly backs. (I often thought that our own good health resulted from frequent and unexpected doses of various sheep drenches and vaccinations. We never suffered from foot rot, overeating disease, tetanus, rabies, or any of the aforementioned parasites.) As each animal was successfully overcome and the dose swallowed, she was given a short spray of red paint across her back to signify one less struggle, or one more triumph, for the Terminator and her helpmate.

Finally, the victims all finished—and by now, like their tormentors, thoroughly exhausted—they streamed out through the opened gate in a creamy wave of billowing fleece while loudly expressing indignation at these outrageous assaults upon their persons. With the scarlet markings on their backs, they always reminded me a bit of a bunch of Hester Prynnes.

There still remained one more job to do, and slowly we would limp over to the rams. These massive but passive creatures, in complete contrast to their wives and daughters, meekly let us have our way with them without so much as a toss of the head or a stamp of a hoof. All they asked for was a good scratching on that particular place at the back of their boss (the part of the horn that stretches across the top of the head). What bliss—oh, what bliss that was!

We tried to repeat OPB once a month, particularly if there had been heavy rain during spring and summer, as damp, muddy ground provides a fertile breeding medium for many parasites, including the meningeal, or brain, worm. As far as I know, to this day this particular parasite has proven immune to any known treatment unless dealt with at an early stage of its ingestion. Our flock would pick it up from the deer droppings in their pasture, and if we could catch this parasite while it was still in the intestine, there was a good chance it might be killed by the worming medication. Once it moved to the brain, paralysis of the spine and the death of the animal resulted. During our shepherding years, we lost three sheep in this cruel way.[1]

Our year's final worming effort took place in mid-October in order to get the flock into the healthiest condition possible for tupping time in mid-November. After this, thankfully, my syringes were washed and put away, the medication shoved to the back of the refrigerator (there either to amuse and/or be a source of consternation to non-regular fridge users), and we all—two- and four-legged inhabitants of Maple Avenue Farm—heaved a huge sigh of relief, which surely could be heard for miles around.

---

[1] We went through this process every year, and whenever the ewes made such a fuss about being dosed, I wished I had been able to communicate to them how lucky they were that it was only done with a syringe. I have never forgotten the graphic worming story my elder sister told me when I was a little girl, only about five years old. Our mother had indicated to us that she would be worming us the next day, and feeling slightly alarmed I (stupidly) asked my sister what this would entail. Big mistake. "Oh," she said, with much relish, "it's a long bit of string with a small mousetrap at the end. You have to swallow it, then it snaps up the worm and Mum pulls it back out. It's excruciatingly painful!" The next day, my poor mother had no idea why I made such an appalling fuss when she called me to come for my "dose." So much for sisterly love!

Ralph Brown

Mabel

A year after we came to Vermont, we were asked to give a home to a very elderly horse. She had belonged to a little girl—the granddaughter of some neighbors—who, tragically, had been killed recently in a road accident.

The mare, Mabel, turned out to be around 35 years of age, really old for a horse. But there was still plenty of life left in the old girl! Age (as I am finding out now) has no place in a life where lush pastures beckon, whether they be real or metaphorical ones. Old Mabel entered our fields like a young filly, kicking up her heels, snorting and galloping around and around, all the while farting merrily.

And how the old mare loved to be ridden. I'm not sure her sight was too good, but she faithfully would follow the horse in front of her and safely carry both myself and our son Hugh (at that time, a beginner rider) on many exciting treks through our surrounding hills and valleys.

Over her first summer with us, all this exercise rounded out her old body with muscle, her coat shone, and she high-stepped from dawn to dusk. One day, returning from an active outing with her, I stopped to talk to Ralph Brown, sitting in the sun outside his milking shed.

"Morning, Ralph," said I, patting Mabel on the neck. "What do you think of the old girl now? Doesn't she look great?"

His blue eyes twinkled. "We-ell," he replied in his gruff voice, "depends on which one you're talking about!"

Haymaking

… good hay, sweet hay, hath no fellow.

—William Shakespeare (*A Midsummer Night's Dream*)

Ready to bale

E VERY SPRING, THE SCENT OF NEW MOWN HAY vividly brings back to me one of life's most nostalgic memories. It never fails to tumble me down through the years to childhood scenes of haymaking.

My first experiences of this age-old work came upon me when I was about five years old, just after the end of World War II. In the summer of 1945, my parents, exhausted after enduring the tumultuous war years in the heart of London, decided to move the family (myself and two older sisters) somewhere peaceful and quiet. We bought a home in the very agricultural county of Kent, known as the Garden of England. The countryside resembled Vermont in many ways, with its gentle hills (no mountains in Kent, though), dense woods, and many wandering streams and rivers. Thus was launched my lifelong love of rural life. To this day I am still fascinated, delighted, and often amused by daily glimpses of both the wild and domesticated worlds around me and cannot conceive of any other type of lifestyle.

In those childhood days, hay was not baled. It was gathered loose into stooks (upright piles of grain or corn stalks) to dry and then stacked into a large hayrick in a sheltered corner of the field, with a roof of straw thatching to keep it dry. My sisters and I loved playing house in the stooks, although, of course, this was not a popular pastime with the farmer, who worried that we would mess up his careful work. One of us was always on guard duty, and when the warning signal was given of approaching danger, we would skedaddle to the nearest hedgerow, there to hide in breathless fear of discovery.

When the hayrick was considered large enough, the remaining stooks were thrown into a huge, creaking wagon drawn by two shire horses, their shaggy hock feathers shaking in rhythm to their solemn plodding steps. The wagon was then driven to the barn and off loaded. We children were allowed to ride on top of the piled hay, and we would burrow deep down into the tawny softness in order to avoid being swept off our lofty perch by the branches overhanging the narrow lane. I know that one always seems to remember happy childhood delights as happening in sunshine, but this one truly did, as that's the only time to make hay!

Haymaking was, of course, a very important activity for us at Maple Avenue Farm. About one-third of our property was put down for this purpose, another third was used for pasture, and the remaining acres were given over to woodland and scrub. As I mentioned in "The Mechanics of Farming," Jim happily spent our first year as farmers visiting various equipment auctions to buy all the necessary machinery, and I got used to the sound of our truck surging its way up the steep farm driveway with some extraordinary metal contraption clattering along behind it.

And so the onset of our second spring at the farm saw all these objects put into use. Jim bravely taught himself how to safely negotiate the various slopes of the four fields that we—with the good advice of neighbor Ralph Brown—decided would give us the best hay yield. Living as we did on such a steep gradient, driving a tractor or truck at what were often forty-five-degree angles required determination, ingenuity, and, especially for a beginner, quite a bit of courage. I was totally amazed at how quickly my husband picked up the various skills necessary for using each piece of the equipment. If there is such a thing as a "natural" hayer, my Jim was certainly it. And what always pleased him so greatly as he progressed from amateur to professional was the approval he gained over the years from the local Vermont farmers, most of whom had had the advantage of practically being born driving a tractor.

There were plenty of learning experiences for me too. No use now my halcyon memories of quiet plodding horses and creaking wagons—oh, no. Now I was the driver of a big GMC truck, which was really scary to maneuver up and down the steeply sloping hayfields. I had to discover how to keep it on an even keel as it became heavier, with more and more bales thrown into the back, and it became more and more unwieldy to steer across the fields. Unlike my husband, I don't think I was in any way a "natural" truck driver, as most of the time my heart was in my mouth with fear that the truck might turn over and roll down one of the steeper slopes.

Depending, of course, on the weather, we usually started cutting the hay about halfway through June. For me, an avid nature and bird enthusiast, the whole haying season included far more than just the actual period of cutting through baling. It started back in May when the grass, just starting to grow, lay quiet and undisturbed save for the undulations created by spring breezes. These vivid green fields were dotted in sublime abundance with the yellows, pinks, whites, oranges, and purples of a myriad of wildflowers. I remember once riding through a field of dandelions in full bloom and being so dazzled that I had to shut my eyes and trust my old mare to carry me quietly along the track and into the shady woods.

And then there were the birdsongs. Years ago, when as a child I ambled around the edges of (never through) English hayfields, I used to listen with such wonder and awe to the exalted songs of the larks, so high in the sky above I could barely see them. (Sadly, larks these days are much endangered, due, as always, to the depredations of mankind.) In these later Vermont years, I came to care also for the ubiquitous, plaintive sound of the wood dove calling from a nearby copse, while from the hayfields came the strange tinny songs of the bobolinks nesting in the growing grasses and the loud *chuck-chuck* of their neighbor nesters, the handsome redwing blackbirds.

After the quiet and bucolic month of May, June arrived and, with luck, produced a spell of hot, dry weather. Suddenly, all those peaceful fields were transformed into places of bustle and noise. Tractors, with different pieces of machinery in tow, droned up and down all day, not only on our hillside but also throughout the valley below, which gradually metamorphosed into a patchwork quilt of different colors and textures. First came the cutting process, which turned the meadow into a flattened, paler version of its former verdant tone. Stage two saw the tedder, with its numerous wild, mechanical arms flailing like a room full of arguing politicians, whirling the drying grass into the dusty air. As the grass came to rest on the ground, it changed the background color of the field to a sage yellow. Then came the sight I loved best, when the drying hay was tidied into strict, beautifully spaced windrows by the officious, organizing rake. Now the meadow took on the aspect of a square of corduroy.

A day or two later (with luck, brisk breezes, and unclouded skies), the hay was well dried out and the Head Honcho of the Haying Equipment—to wit, the formidable-looking baler—made its grand entrance. With what gusto this big machine sucked up the sun-baked grass into its maw and, after much clanking, bobbing, and grinding, delivered at last from its nether end a neat, oblong package tied up with string, quite remi-

Baler trouble!

niscent of a birthday present. Round and round went the tractor pulling this mechanical marvel, leaving, by early evening, rows of bales lined up across the empty stubble.

During the baling process, there was always a nagging worry as to whether the baler (ours was old and known to be a temperamental machine) would perform its functions correctly. Would it tie the bales tightly enough and would its knotting process work perfectly? Bad knotting produced loose bales (scornfully pointed out by my haying crew as "loosies"), which were a real bane as they tended to fall apart during loading and upset the careful stacking in the truck. Most were returned to the windrows to be re-baled.

On top of the worry about the condition of the bales was the concern that the engine baler itself might break down. One afternoon, not only did our baler die a sudden death but so did two others brought over by kind farming friends (Steve Wetmore and Carelton Phelps) to help us finish gathering in the bales. Finally, after the third "death," in desperation we called another of our neighbors, Dwayne Lawrence. At once he bustled over with his huge tractor and baler and cleaned up our field lickety-split. Of course, all these balers lying around in various attitudes of disablement meant that our baler savior, Ralph Whitney, had some real problems on his hands. These he tackled and solved with his never-failing enthusiasm for the internal intricacies of farm machinery.

As opposed to all these worries, there were also pleasures attached to these haying days. Often I would take our three dogs and a picnic lunch (dog biscuits included, of course) up to the field that Jim was currently working on. The five of us would rest in the shade of the woods' edge and contentedly munch our food. Jim might tell me of the small, dappled fawn he glimpsed, startled from its safe hiding place in the middle of the field, running to the woods for safety. Or of the hungry vixen waiting to pounce on the frightened voles hurriedly evacuating their now endangered nests from the long grass. On a lucky day, we might observe a red-tailed hawk wheeling lazily high up in the pale blue sky, his ringing cry loud in the stillness of the midday heat. From the nearby stone wall, chipmunks scolded us for invading their territory. Luckily for these cheeky little animals, the dogs were more interested in our sandwiches than in addressing rodent temerity. Loath to leave our cool and peaceful sanctuary, we prolonged our lunch break by plucking our dessert—a stalk of grass from which we unwrapped the outer layer and sucked out the moist sweetness of its inner stem.

Since our equipment was very old-fashioned, we usually needed three or four days of good hot sunshine to complete the whole job, from the cutting to the stacking in the barn. Rain before the hay was dry meant either a totally ruined field or hay that needed to be re-tedded and re-raked, a repeat process that resulted in very inferior hay. This second-class fodder was usually spurned by our spoilt flock, and all hell broke loose until a better class of hay was produced. The rejected food was then passed on to our horses, who had a far less demanding palate. The opposite side to rainy weather was the dread that the temperature might be in the nineties, thus making our work a real misery.

Either of these conditions affected my part in the haymaking. I was in charge of the pickup and transport of the bales down to the barn. For this, I needed a crew of three or four willing workers. On a good day, I would be able to find and hire enough, but occasionally brave friends or unsuspecting guests had to be drafted for the job. (I could rarely tap them a second time.) A crew of four strong youngsters was ideal. One would stay up in the hayfield and "bunch" the bales together into piles, making the job of picking them up much quicker and easier; two boys were needed to throw the bales into the truck; and one stayed down at the barn to stack them therein—the least popular work, as it was always so hot inside. (Traditionally, the youngest and least experienced lad got stuck with this task.)

Getting the bales in is an exhausting task, with the chaff swirling in the hot, often humid air, sticking to sweaty skin and clogging the nares—certainly not work for the weak in body or spirit. Even driving the truck alongside the shady hedgerows brought welcome relief from the burning sun. Often, while down at the barn to unload the bales, my boys would use the hose to cool off their outer selves while I dashed into the village to bring back ice cream to cool their inner selves.

But sometimes we were lucky; the temperature dropped into the seventies and a fresh breeze kept us all cool. Then it was breathtakingly beautiful up there on the mountain and so utterly timeless, with the river

Here comes the first bale!

meandering lazily through the valley below and, far beyond that, the familiar, well-loved hills and mountains rising and falling and folding into the hazy purple distance. It was such a pleasure to watch my team heft the bales into the truck with youthful vigor and to listen idly to their gossip and repartee.

There was always a little rivalry between the different teams as to how many bales could be stacked on the truck. I think the record was seventy, set by Jeremiah Linehan. However, this high and heavy a load made the task of getting the truck down our precipitous stony track very hazardous. Though my personal preference for loading was the old Vermont way, told to me by my friend Charlie Brown—"bale tight, load light, run like hell"—I knew my role as driver was a very humble one, so I never made any comments, just did what I was told. My workers, being teenagers, thought they knew everything, but I'd notice how quiet everyone got as we inched down the hill and the tension mounted over whether the load would topple and the wearisome task of reloading would have to take place. So, I did have the final quiet little chuckle to myself.

If weather, machinery, and crew availability were all cooperative, we got in two cuttings each year. The first, bigger main crop was harvested in June and July, and the second in August. This second crop, a shorter and more tender-stalked harvest, is known by the New England name of rowen, and this we gave to the ewes after they had given birth. And, oh, how they loved it!

Finally, came the triumphant evening in late August when the last bale was joyfully thrown into the full barn, the last hayer paid off and thanked profusely, and all the machinery was stowed in the equipment shed. Jim and I, exhausted but tremendously relieved, would gaze up our hill with joyful satisfaction at the closely shaven fields, smug in the knowledge that within our huge barn, the sweet-smelling stacks stretched up into the dusky heights of the vaulted roof. The long winter months were well provided for. Then we would wend our weary way through the gloaming to our house to put our feet up on the cool front porch and sip a couple of tankards of that most divine of drinks—a cold, cold beer.

Helping hands (and hooves?) loading the truck

Saint Fred (bottom step) and Bessie supervising (top step)

Saint Fred, the Singing Dog

Fred came to us one...yes, one dark and stormy night. I was returning home through lashing rain. Luckily, I was driving very slowly because of poor visibility. Suddenly, my headlights picked up something brown in the middle of the road. A fox? Too small. A dog? Yes! As I got out of the car, it came running up to me. It looked like a cross between a bull terrier and—who knows?—perhaps a beagle. No collar. Well, there was no way I could leave him there in the rain, so onto the backseat of the car he happily hopped and proceeded to "sing" to me all the way home!

And so Fred joined the gang at Maple Avenue Farm. No one ever claimed him, and how glad that made us. He was a most cheerful and loving dog although somewhat of a scrapper, as are most terriers. In this he was aided and abetted by Bessie—herself, of course, a terrier and quite partial to a bit of a set-to. She would actively encourage Fred to scrap with other dogs foolish enough to come too near our farm by yapping furiously, bouncing up and down, and feinting little forays towards the arguing dogs, always being very careful to keep well out of range of any trouble that might spill over onto her. So it was always poor Fred who got into trouble for scrapping, while Bess sat in the background looking smug. He never seemed to mind our scolding too much and patiently waited for the next opportunity for a bit of pugilistic excitement to present itself.

But above all, Fred loved singing. He would sing with guests while they had their early morning tea in bed; he would sing with us while we read our books in the evening; he would sing on car journeys. One memorable evening, Fred sang a very special blessing in beautiful harmony with the Reverend William Sloan Coffin, who happened to be having dinner with us. After this episode, Fred joined the august company of our farm's other saint, Ralph Whitney, and became known as Saint Fred of Grannyhand Hill.

Darling Fred was also a wonderful sous chef and delighted in his job of replacing the first dishwasher cycle and doing the "pre-wash" himself. But, alas, his efficiency led to his girth becoming larger and larger, and despite many attempts on our part to find a good diet food—and firing him from his chosen career—we could not solve his weight problem. One morning, he accidentally fell off his favorite sofa and, because of his heaviness, fatally damaged his spine. His rear end became paralyzed. Despite heroic efforts by our veterinarian to reverse the damage, nothing could be done. To our great sadness, Saint Fred's time with us came to an end.

I still miss his optimistic presence.

THE SEMEN KING

Nothing is so difficult but that it may be

found out by seeking.

—Publius Terentius Afer (*Heautontimoroumenos*)

Beautiful examples from our Scottish Blackface flock.

OVER THE YEARS, WE WORKED HARD TO BUILD UP A FLOCK commensurate with Scottish blackface breed guidelines: straight backed, strong shouldered, widely spread horns, and an imposing arched Roman nose. These sheep are much prized in Great Britain for their wool, used in the production of Scottish tweed and top-of-the-line Axminster-brand carpets. Their meat is also in much demand, being very lean and tasty.

Although we used our flock for both these attributes, our main line of business was breeding simply to sell to folks who liked the breed. The fact that Scotties are a minor breed in this country and therefore not easily obtained helped to give us a good and nationwide market. The downside of being a minor breed was that finding new and good-looking sires and dams was difficult. We had to constantly widen our search for new bloodlines to prevent inbreeding.

One year, to our consternation, we found we had finally reached an impasse. Wide as we spread our net for stock with different genes, we could find little of interest in America. Even the Mount Saviour Monastery, because they had reduced their flock size, had nothing to offer us. Then Fate stepped in with a helping hand.

We were on an October visit to my sister in Wiltshire, England. One brisk, sunny day, I walked to a nearby prehistoric site, the Avebury stone circle. These great sarsen (sandstone) boulders, some weighing more than forty tons, stand in a huge circle, rather like petrified Knights of the Round Table. I've always found this place a fascinating and quite mystical place. On this late fall morning it was almost deserted, and I strode from boulder to boulder possessed by a feeling of tremendous awe for my Bronze Age ancestors. Then, topping a small rise, what should I see below me peacefully grazing in and out among these giant stones? A flock of Scottish blackface sheep. And what sheep! Beautiful, wide, soaring horns and backs as straight as a tabletop. I stood and watched their placid meanderings, wishing fervently that I could put the whole flock in an airplane and fly them home to Vermont.

Filled with excitement, I ran back to my sister's house to tell Jim and bring him to see this newly discovered treasure. For a brief while, we were totally carried away with dreams of these beautiful creatures adorning our green Vermont hillside.

Next day, however, as we attempted to turn our dreams into reality and telephoned various government offices, we were brought sadly back to earth. Rules for importing sheep into the United States were prohibitive. First, one had to bring the animals into Canada, leave them there for five years, and only then was there hope that the U.S. Department of Agriculture would give permission to import the beasts into this country. However, there was (and probably still is to this day) a reason for this long delay in being able to take possession of one's imports. That is scrapie, the ovine equivalent of bovine spongiform encephalopathy (BSE), more commonly known as mad cow disease. Scrapie does not manifest itself until a sheep is four or five years old, so testing a young animal would yield no answer as to whether the disease was present and therefore unfit for human consumption. Hence, the long quarantine time. For us, with our small sheep operation, this five-year period represented a very expensive and long-term project. And we still urgently needed new genes for our upcoming breeding season.

Shortly after our return from England, an answer came to me in the proverbial middle of the night. Nudging Jim awake, I said excitedly to him, "Semen! That's what we need!" A few moments of confusion then reigned, contributed to by sharp complaints from Bessie the Jack Russell, fast asleep under the blankets and very annoyed at being awoken from rat-killing dreams. Hastily I explained to my dazed but eager husband that I hadn't been visited by a sudden and overpowering urge for his body but that I was talking much more prosaically about sheep. Sitting up in bed, I eagerly ranted on. "If we can't import the actual animal, maybe we can import ram semen from Scotland or some other country and artificially inseminate our ewes. Perhaps that would be cheaper anyway."

So thrilled were we at this new idea that we talked until the first rays of the rising sun tinged the hillside across the valley with a luminous pearly pink. Jim could hardly wait to start this new project rolling. Poor innocents that we were, we had not the slightest concept of the reels of bureaucratic red tape that he was to struggle through in the ensuing months.

First, in what was to be an endless series of telephone calls, Jim contacted Britain's Ministry of Agriculture, an organization that, judging from the medieval slowness of most of its departments, was still mired in the nineteenth century. He was constantly forwarded from office to office, which never seemed to contain the necessary official. My poor husband was nearly always told to "please hold on and I'll try and find him," at which statement I laughed and said it probably meant that the person in question was out indulging in that time-honored and time-consuming British tradition of a morning "cuppa," more formally known as a cup of tea. But Jim was determined to accomplish his mission. Finally (oh, happy day!), a very haughty voice grudgingly agreed that the ministry could send to Vermont the forms necessary for dealing with the import of ram semen to the USA.

Luckily, this continuing drama was being played out over the winter months, a moderately idle time in farm life. Weeks passed before the long-awaited package arrived, only to reveal contents that dealt with permission to import bull, not ram, semen. Back to the phone again. By now, Jim had also come up with some other promising leads: a private firm in Scotland that dealt in the semen export business; a company in Idaho that had stocks from many different breeds, including Scottish blackface; and a tip that Ireland's Department of Agriculture might be more helpful.

He was kept very busy. E-mails flew back and forth. Forms rolled off our fax machine. Letters arrived daily from all over the world, including England, Ireland, Australia, New Zealand and Canada. The phone rang constantly. I would fall asleep at night with Jim engrossed in books and pamphlets describing the benefits of artificial insemination (or A.I., in more common usage) for sheep, probably an experience unique to a farmer's wife.

Our lives became dominated by this search, and many of our friends began to view us with suspicion. I startled a friend who was visiting with me in the kitchen one morning when, after answering the telephone, I went to the back door and yelled to Jim, "There's a man on the phone who wants to talk to you about your semen." My friend finished her coffee in one gulp and beat a hasty retreat, obviously fearing to intrude on what she perceived as a very personal matter. Even our children, when telephoning home, started asking to speak to The Semen King.

Months went by, and finally we had to face the discouraging facts. We could import a ram directly from Ireland but the cost of shipping the animal was too high for our modest budget. We could import semen from Scotland or buy it from a company in Idaho, but we had to buy twenty straws (a straw contains enough semen to inseminate one ewe) at the high cost of $90 per straw, and all the straws came from the same ram. In the long run, having all of our eighteen ewes bred to the same sire would do nothing to diversify the flock's gene pool. Lastly, if we did decide on A.I., the best way to do it was by laparoscopy, inserting the semen directly into the ewe's uterus by means of a minor surgical procedure. More telephone calls yielded only one veterinarian who could perform this operation, and he lived in California. Moreover, he was not willing to come east for a mere eighteen animals—or only at devastating expense.

We did eventually import a ram from Ottawa, Canada, a vigorous and efficient chap. General Montcalm proceeded quickly to create a new bloodline.

Later, after this whole debacle was over, Jim and I amused ourselves with the following discussion: what would our "girls'" opinions have been on the matter of A.I.? We always loved to anthropomorphize our animals, be they sheep, horses, dogs or ducks. (Not Lloyd—we really didn't want to know Lloyd's opinions on life!) And how we laughed about their following imaginary conversation:

> "My dear Marilyn, I will not take kindly to a strange man taking weird liberties with my person. I think we should go down into the village and march past Coburns' General Store in protest. My placard will read, Real Ewes Want Real Rams."

> "You're absolutely right, Ullambana. And my sign shall read, Bye-bye, A.I."

Had we proceeded with our A.I. idea, I think Jim and I would have had a mutton mutiny on our hands.

Honeybees

Sweet is every sound,
Sweeter thy voice, but every sound is sweet;
Myriads of rivulets hurrying through the lawn,
The moan of doves in immemorial elms,
And murmuring of innumerable bees.
—Alfred, Lord Tennyson, 1809–1892

My first hive

"And murmuring of innumerable bees." How I have always loved this reference to the honeybee. It is so apt and so resonant and a much better description of their sound than "buzz" or "drone." And the day came when I realized how very fitting a description it was.

As well as a variety of animals that kept company with us on the farm, we had insects too—honeybees, to be precise. About five years after our move north, I decided to become a beekeeper. It is a pleasure that I still pursue to this day. Although there is so much to know and learn about these extraordinary little creatures, for now, alas! I only have room to give a very simple introduction to their way of life.

Honeybees, *Apis mellifera*, are among this planet's most miraculous and intelligent beings, having a highly sophisticated social structure, as do ants and termites. Human beings would do well to emulate the honeybees' way of life. Their lives are not about competition with their fellows but about group cooperation.

Relocating the hive to a sunnier situation.

Honeybees perform an absolutely necessary function to our world—agriculture and natural—by pollinating plants, trees, and wildflowers, thereby continuing nature's food chain and humanity's future here on earth. A great deal of all the food that humans eat is pollinated by bees. Sadly, as with so many species today, these tiny creatures are becoming increasingly endangered by disease.

Many people, especially children, are frightened of bees or what they perceive to be a bee. But the honeybee, unlike her cousin the wasp, is a defensive insect and will only sting to protect herself or her hive. Those pesky little buzzers spoiling your picnic will almost surely be a wasp.

A bee colony can number up to 60,000 bees at peak honey-flow time and is made up of three types of bees: the workers, sterile females that constitute 98 percent of the colony; the drones; and, most importantly, the queen bee, the layer of eggs. A queen can live for up to three years, and in return for a lifetime of producing progeny to maintain the hive, she is fed, pampered, and guarded by her worker daughters.

The worker bees are well named. As well as Looking After Mother, many of them (they are also called scout bees) forage all spring, summer, and fall for pollen—nectar to feed their young and to make the honey that will sustain their hive through the coming winter—and also sap and resins from trees. The sap is mixed with enzymes into a substance called propolis, which is used to seal the hive and make it weatherproof (very important in cold winter climes like Vermont) and to make repairs around their home. It is indeed a busy life.

In contrast to their hardworking mother and sterile sisters, the lives of drones appear to be idyllic—at first glance, that is. In actual fact, the idyll is somewhat flawed. Drones are part of a hive purely to impregnate the queen on her mating flights in the springtime. After these swarmings are over, the drones live the life of Riley for all the following summer. They just laze around the hive doing nothing but eating, fed by their long-suffering sisters. But, aha! when the cold weather approaches, their existence becomes a very different story. Those same obliging sister bees, realizing that with winter coming the drones are of no further use to the hive and can only be a burden on their society, throw them all out to die of cold and starvation. Rather a Shakespearean ending, I think.

How industrious, how brilliant, how astonishingly clever, how absorbing is the life of the *Apis mellifera*! I wish I could tell you more about them right now; perhaps I'll have to write another book. I hope, however, that even with this short synopsis, I may have inspired you to become a beekeeper yourself. The honeybees and the planet surely need you.

For so work the honey-bees,
creatures that by a rule in nature teach
the act of order to a peopled kingdom.
—William Shakespeare (*Henry V*)

TUPPING DAY

… an old black ram is tupping your white ewe.

—William Shakespeare (*Othello*)

Spring lambs in the making!

"T
UPPING" IS A WORD USED BY SHEPHERDS in the north of England and Scotland. It is derived from the French tuper, "to top," and describes (very succinctly, don't you think?) the act of procreation between a ram, known as the tup, and a ewe.

At Maple Avenue Farm, the rams were put in to mate the ewes on November 15. This lively annual event was known as Tupping Day and could be said to be the most important day of our farming year. As with many festivals (which we considered Tupping Day to be), we prepared for it weeks in advance. First the eanlings, the six-month-old ewe lambs who were too young to be bred, were separated from the main flock. Then the rams were moved as far away as possible from their potential mates.

It was of the utmost importance not to allow a fence jumper to get loose with the as yet unbred ewes. Such a disaster would completely nullify our careful breeding charts and we would be unable to use or sell the resultant progeny as pure Scottish blackface. The rams' field began to take on the aspect of Alcatraz as we strengthened it against breakouts. Where the field was bordered by electric wire, the wire was tightened and sometimes extra strands added. In places where there was board or stock wire, gaps were checked for and filled in with old doors, old metal gates, and, one year in an extreme emergency, a tree trunk. But none of our precautions stopped the constant patrol along the fence line by these future sires as the autumn breeze wafted the delicious scent of ewes in estrus (sexual readiness) across the dividing pastures. We fence maintainers also observed much macho posturing, pawing of the ground, and clashing of their huge horny bosses as they staged mock, and sometimes not-so-mock, fights.

The intended brides, meanwhile, grazed unconcernedly in their field, obviously enjoying the extra grain ration served to them each evening to get them into top condition for November 15, or T-day. All the ewes, that is, except for Dorothy.

Dorothy was raised by friends as a family pet and was given to us when they felt she needed her own kind of company. She was not a Scottish blackface but a ewe of unknown breeding, decidedly overweight, and extremely homely of visage, and her sturdy silhouette stood out glaringly against the elegant outlines of her Scottie flock mates. But Dorothy was convinced she was Mata Hari incarnate. While the other ewes neither knew nor appeared to care about the passionate activities that shortly awaited them, Dorothy did care. She spent her days and nights bleating enticingly to the boys, forcing them into an even more frantic inspection of their ramparts. (When the Great Day came and the brides and grooms were finally put together, Dorothy was the first to demand and get attention, proving—to muddle an old saying—that rams do make passes at ewes with wide asses.)

Finally, with the rams (hopefully) safely enclosed, Jim and I shifted from being prison makers to being marriage brokers. We spent long hours compiling lists of which female would go to which sire, searching through bloodlines, and discussing the distinctive merits of each animal. We usually kept three rams, who each bred, on average, six ewes. This isn't much of a harem for a single ram; in bigger flocks, one ram could be expected to service up to one hundred or two hundred ewes. However, our enterprise was small and we only ran about eighteen to twenty breeding ewes. We finally arrived at this number (somewhat by trial and error) as moderately easy for us to manage efficiently.

Besides working on keeping the rams apart from the ewes at this time during our first breeding year, Jim and I discovered there was another preparation to be organized. At the time of breeding our flock for the first time, we didn't know beans about the business and tried to do everything according to the book—literally, a manual called *Raising Sheep the Modern Way*. One suggestion therein was to put a breeding harness on the ram while he was in with his ewes. This harness holds a large piece of colored chalk, in shepherd's parlance known as a *raddle*, on the ram's chest so that when he mounts a ewe, the color rubs off on her backside and shows that she has been mated. By counting forward the requisite 145 to 154 days, we could calculate roughly when her lamb(s) would be born the following April. This first year, however, we learned that very often a book does not always explain processes adequately.

Early on the morning of our first Tupping Day, Jim and I, harness in hand, advanced upon the rams' field. Our tups preferred to first face the daily challenges of fence breaching and fighting rivals with a long, peaceful cud-chewing lie-in. Therefore, we were able to artfully pounce upon one unsuspecting male before he had time to connect our arrival with danger. The idyllic early morning scene changed abruptly as Lover Boy objected with great indignation to having the harness put on him. Perhaps he felt it would impede his style with the ladies. To add to our difficulties, the harness turned out to be a veritable octopus of straps and buckles, impossible to fit on an ovine determined to act like a bronco.

It was then that a brilliant idea flashed through my mind. I turned to Jim and said, "Let's try it on you first and then maybe we can figure things out more easily." My poor husband looked both alarmed and doubtful.

"We-ell, if you really feel it would help…"

Poor man! But being a patient soul, he submitted himself to my idea with quiet dignity while I fiddled, pulled, stretched, and somehow finally fastened the fearsome contraption around him. Standing back in triumph to survey the red raddle glowing brightly from his chest, I said with a giggle, "I hope I won't see any of the ladies in the village sporting red backsides!"

At that moment, a voice behind us said, "Morning, folks."

I whirled around. Jim, of course, had to remain stationary, swathed as he was in ram harness. There stood Ralph Brown. Now, being a true gentleman, he tactfully ignored these very peculiar goings-on of his neighbors and went on to talk of the reason for his visit.

Meanwhile, Jim and I, and it would certainly be fitting to say somewhat sheepishly, endeavored clumsily to disentangle ourselves from our embarrassing situation. That harness went straight on the rubbish heap.

Old Ralph never mentioned what he'd observed, but every November he always asked how tupping was progressing, and those blue eyes twinkled with suppressed humor.

Now, back to the dramatic events unfolding on the hillside of Maple Avenue Farm.

Dance cards indicating which ram was to squire which ewe were now completed, separate pens were all ready to receive the various groups, and friends were gathered together to help with the proceedings. The fun could begin.

First, the ewes were brought into a central holding area. As each one was caught, her ear-tag number was called out and she was dispatched to the appropriate enclosure where, in a while, her designated tup would join her little group. Since Scottish blackfaces are naturally very clannish, each ewe resisted both vocally and physically to being separated from her sisters. As our sweating helpers dived and grabbed and tried to avoid being trampled on by sharp little hooves, the whole scene became reminiscent of some sort of wild rodeo, and I could see our volunteers were beginning to heartily regret what seemed like an offer to help with an intriguing project. But at last this part of the grand plan was finished, and we all had a much-needed breather in the form of coffee and donuts.

Now came the dramatic Grand Finale as the more-than-willing bridegrooms were brought forth. As our rams trotted down the road to their woolly paradise, I always felt this was a time when there should be a loud blaring of trumpets, something along the lines of the "Grand March" from Verdi's opera *Aida* or, at the very least, the strains of Mendelssohn's "Wedding March." How splendid they looked, with their massive curved horns proudly out-splayed, huge low-hung "ramhood" swaying ponderously, upper lip raised to better receive the inviting scents of their future mates. There's a gland under this upper lip that exudes a chemical substance called pheromone. This serves as a stimulus to the opposite sex of the breed (not needed by Dorothy, of course). One of the first signs in August that our ewes were sexually ready was this raised upper lip in the rams, who would catch a whiff of the delights that awaited them across the meadows come fall and the arrival of Tupping Day.

As we opened each gate and let the ram in with his breeding team, there was a general rushing and milling about. Then some lucky lady, obviously at the right stage of readiness, got singled out. Round and round and up and down the ram paraded his ewe. Ovine wooing is short but sweet, with a very polite and loving period of nuzzling and low utterings before consummation is attempted. Since this final denouement usually happened modestly during the night hours, Jim and I would always be a little concerned that there had been any real action. Of course, the raddle harness would have helped calm these concerns, but using it was obviously no longer a considered option.

However, the following April, our lack of tupping faith was proved groundless. As we watched with delight a plethora of beautifully healthy lambs running and leaping in our pastures, there was ample evidence (Dorothy being the first to provide it!) that both our rams and ewes were very fertile. Once again, proof had been provided that those November nights five months before had indeed been spent in passionate abandon.

WINTER

Dinner time

TUPPING DAY WAS ALMOST THE LAST BIG ACTIVITY AT MAPLE AVENUE FARM. Only one more chore remained to be accomplished at the end of November. This was the day Jim and I most dreaded in the whole year: taking the surplus ram lambs to slaughter. The better-looking ones had been sold earlier in the year for breeding stock, leaving about ten to twelve young males who were sold for meat.

Some farmers took their beasts to the slaughterhouse the day before the arranged date, but we didn't want our sheep spending their last night in a strange, frightening place. So we rose early on the fateful day, quietly loaded the rams onto the truck, and drove them to a little Vermont slaughterhouse down the road. It was a small comfort to us to know there was very little waiting time for our animals; usually, within an hour of their arrival they were gone.

Many, many times we were asked, "How can you eat animals you knew and had nurtured for nearly a year?" The answer always was, and still is, "How can anyone eat an animal that has led a tortured life and ended with a painful and terrifying death?" It is one of the realities of farming that you eat what you raise. And perhaps the difference between Jim and me sitting down to a winter meal of lamb chops and someone doing the same in a restaurant is that we had an intimate and very real appreciation not just for the meal but also for the life and well-being of the animal.

Our lives now quieted. Snow fell with all its beauty and silence, a happening that never seemed to trouble the sheep. We went up to feed them after a big storm to find only their heads sticking out from the snow, feet tucked snugly under their thick fleeces. The horses spent more time in their warm stables, stamping impatiently as they waited for their thrice daily hay feedings. The wild birds flocked to the bird feeders. Fox footprints marched across the white landscape. And the annual battles with icy conditions on our steep road from the valley commenced.

In the house, dogs (including, of course, Churchill) vied for the coziest positions next to the woodstove. Jim and I began to finish up the many household tasks that had been neglected for most of the past year. We were able to enjoy tranquil times with each other again. We started to read through our piles of neglected books. We visited with, and were visited by, friends; took in a few movies; went on a few trips; and, over the darkened months, talked at length about our plans for the coming year on Maple Avenue Farm.

It was a time of rest and recuperation—a lovely, gentle time for thought, not action. A slower pace of life altogether and a much needed respite for us both.

Until, that is, spring came again.

Winter landscape

BEGIN AT THE BEGINNING,
AND GO ON TILL YOU COME TO THE END

—Lewis Carroll (*Alice's Adventures in Wonderland*)

So how should I end this book about such an intense, lively, and fascinating period of our lives? Perhaps the best way would be with a quote by writer-naturalist Henry Beston that I love and appreciate for its simple truth:

The animal shall not be measured by man. In a world older
and more complete than ours they move finished and complete,
gifted with extensions of the senses we have lost or never attained,
living by voices we shall never hear. They are not brethren,
they are not underlings; they are other nations, caught with ourselves
in the net of life and time, fellow prisoners of the splendor
and travail of the earth.

(from *The Outermost House*)

EPILOGUE

Time is a sort of river of passing events,

and strong is its current; no sooner is a thing

brought to sight than it is swept by and another

takes its place, and this too shall be swept away.

—Marcus Aurelius Antoninus, 121–180 BCE

WE LIVED AT MAPLE AVENUE FARM FOR NIGH ON TWENTY YEARS. Towards the end of that time, Jim's health became increasingly fragile. We came to the sad and reluctant decision that managing the farm was just becoming too difficult for us. We would have to leave.

My one remaining horse, Bronwyn, all the sheep, and even Lloyd were given to suitable and loving homes. The machinery and equipment went back to the auctions from whence it originally had come. We were lucky to discover and purchase a lovely little cottage near the village, perfectly suited to our new and simplified lifestyle. The dogs, of course, as well as my beehive, would accompany us to our new home.

And so, for the last time one sunny May morning, we drove away from our now silent house and pastures, down our familiar steep, tree-lined avenue, our hearts too full to even begin to express a small fraction of the myriad of memories we took with us.

Two years later, as dawn tinged the snowy December landscape with rose and gold, my beloved Jim slipped peacefully away.

* * * * *

I continue to live at the cottage, in close harmony with all my wild friends—the deer, foxes, skunks, coyotes, field mice, snakes, an enormous woodchuck (whom I've named Arnie Schwarzenegger), and birds of every color and voice. And thanks to the generosity of the friends to whom we gifted her when we left the farm, I still ride Bronwyn. Both of us are now considerably older and creakier but are always able to enjoy each other's company, journeying through the quiet woods and fields. Each springtime I fill with excitement when I receive calls from fellow shepherds asking me to come and help them with a difficult lambing, a task I love and still miss greatly.

I hope you have enjoyed this book about Maple Avenue Farm and all its happy reminiscences as much as I have loved writing it. Perhaps some of you will be encouraged to become shepherds.

I can thoroughly recommend the life!

GLOSSARY

Banamine: painkiller/anti-inflamatory drug

billhook: cutting/pruning tool with a hooked blade

bolus: a large pill, mostly given orally, occasionally anally

Bucephalus: Alexander the Great's magnificent charger (horse)

cognomen: name, nickname

colustrum: milk secreted by a mother for a few days after birthing, characterized by high-protein and anti-body content; very important for the health of the baby (or, as in this book, lamb)

dressage: the execution by a trained horse of precision movements in response to barely perceptible signals from its rider

hock feathers: the long hair growing from the back of a horse's hocks (the joints in animals corresponding to the human ankle)

maw: stomach, or suggestive of the throat of a voracious animal (the latter description will be more understood after reading this book!)

Murphy's Law: an observation that anything that can go wrong, will go wrong; named after engineer Edward Murphy, 1917–1958

nares: nostrils or nasal passages

pig in the middle: game played with three people, similar to "keep away" in the U.S.

Prynne, Hester: central character in Nathanial Hawthorne's book *The Scarlet Letter*, forced to wear a red "A" on her clothing for committing adultery

shire horse: large, strong draught horse

ted/tedder: machine for turning and spreading new mown hay so it will dry

Trakehner: breed of large, powerful saddle horses that originated in East Prussia and excel in dressage

wool pool: an event that took place once a year in the summer months. Shepherds from all over Vermont would bring their full wool bags, which were then loaded into a huge van and sold at, presumably, a wool auction. We were so glad to be rid of these huge bags that we were not too interested in what happened to them.

ACKNOWLEDGEMENTS

"… I thank you for your voices: thank you:

Your most sweet voices"

—Shakespeare (*Coriolanus*)

It would be impossible to thank individually the many, many people who have encouraged, advised, and inspired me over the nearly fifteen years it has taken to bring *Love Among the Lambs* to fruition. However, I would like to acknowledge the unique help that some of you have afforded me.

My children, Hugh and Melanie Finn, for guidance with some "sticky" bits.

My niece, Elizabeth Shealy, for her never-failing faith in this project.

Our families and friends, who so willingly pitched in to help on many occasions—and still kept coming back to visit!

Jessica Swift of Swift Ink Editorial Services, for her invaluable and enthusiastic encouragement and guidance on my early efforts.

Joe Medlicott, who first introduced me to the dreaded "red pencil" and then taught me to appreciate it!

Martha Manheim, for her early editing of some very raw writing.

My wonderful writers group—Ruth, Anne, Pat, and Randy—who, over four years, patiently listened, advised, corrected, and endorsed each chapter.

Dorian Yates, herself an inspiration and a fantastic and generous fount of wise and comforting advice on the publication of one's "masterpiece"!

Anita Warren of Getting Ink Done—editor *par excellence*—for her incredible patience, skill, and sense of humor in making sense of a rather homespun text.

Sandra Smith-Ordway, for her expert handling of the "fun" part of *Love Among the Lambs*—that of designing this book exactly as I had always envisioned it.

Mark Shaw, who worked his magic on all my photographs, many of which were old and faded.

The Norwich Bookstore (that small corner of paradise), for their unquestioning belief in my abilities.

And, lastly, I would like to remember my parents, Colin and Sheila Porteous, without whose generosity this book would not have come into being.

To each and all of you and to many other unmentioned "sweet voices," my unfailing gratitude for allowing me to make a lifelong dream come true.

A portion of funds from the sale of this book will go to the Humane Farming Association.

But one man loved the pilgrim soul in you,

And loved the sorrows of your changing face;

—William Butler Yeats ("When You Are Old")